S0-AVG-575

MASTER TEACHER
NADIA BOULANGER

Nadia Boulanger, 1935.

MASTER
TEACHER

DON G. CAMPBELL

THE PASTORAL PRESS

WASHINGTON, D.C.

THE PASTORAL PRESS
225 Sheridan Street, NW
Washington, DC 20011

The Pastoral Press is the publications division
of the National Association of Pastoral
Musicians, a membership organization of
musicians and clergy dedicated to fostering
the art of musical liturgy.

Printed in the United States of America

ISBN 0-912405-03-1

DEDICATION

For my parents, who took me to Fontainebleau

There is no sharp line of demarcation between the music of today and the music of yesterday. Music, like life, is in constant evolution. Its transformation goes on incessantly, but the process is so gradual that, for the most part, we remain quite unconscious of the nature and extent of the changes which are taking place before our very eyes. We are too inattentive, our minds too passive, to observe or record, to say nothing of understanding them. It is so much easier to rest contented with what we have already acquired than to change ever so slightly those routine but profound habits of thought and feeling which govern our life, and by which we live so blissfully. This mental inertia is, perhaps, our greatest enemy. Insidiously it leads us to assume that we can renew our lives without renewing our habits.

NADIA BOULANGER

January 27, 1925

Contents

Foreword

Istand before a statue, sacred to some, revered by many, respected by generations. It speaks for itself, not of itself. It is of an ingenious quality, an abstract power, a practical design. As a Zen monk will not discuss the power of the riddles of freedom, this statue cannot be easily defined.

Nadia Boulanger warned me in 1976 about approaching the reality of preparing this book:

> *The more I measure the generosity and the extent of your purpose, dear Don, the more anxious I feel. Indisputably, I must help you with your purpose. I must help you realize your plans. But you must realize that I am, not generalizing, but trying to face the reality of each day and each person. I am terrified to let you create a real deception of my life.*

I was warned by every person I interviewed, by their indirect variety of impressions. Mademoiselle saw that words taken out of context could be meaningless and misleading. She seldom wrote comments on music in the form of articles. She refused to write books, knowing their possibilities of misunderstanding. Most of the articles included in this book written by Nadia Boulanger were written early in her career. Her attitudes and views evolved throughout her life and she would have changed some of her perspectives in print.

MASTER TEACHER is neither a biography, nor a scrapbook, but rather a collection of impressions and reflections. It is aimed at the indefinable, quintessential elements of her remarkable life.

As a thirteen-year-old, I met Mademoiselle Boulanger at the American Conservatory in Fontainebleau in 1960. I went there to study piano with Jean Casadesus. During the two full years I stayed in Paris and Fontainebleau, I sang in Mademoiselle's ensembles, attended her general classes and took a course in keyboard harmony. As my musical world awakened, the presence of her mind, manners, and intentions made lasting impressions on me. As my own career developed, her inspiration continued to extend and have a marked importance in my teaching.

The art spirit that lived in Nadia Boulanger was not a crystalized form, but a fluid and resonant energy. That energy is placed in jeopardy when put into a written form. I face that challenge.

Nadia Boulanger refused to speak of herself, her inner views, her personal history. Toward the end of her life, a series of interviews by the public media in France and Great Britain penetrated part of her resistance. She was never convinced that her life, her associations, and her musical ideas should be reformed into an intact statement. It is ironically curious that Igor Stravinsky's *Memoires and Commentaries* is dedicated to her.

The spoken words of Nadia Boulanger were at times unique and profound. At other times, they reflected the century in which she was born. Her wisdom echoes the sympathetic depth of many other artists, yet found its power in the context and circumstance of teaching. No other woman in the history of music parallels her influence. A pure definition of her is elusive.

The scores of friends, students, and associates who have assisted with the materials used in this book are gratefully thanked. Their time, their libraries, and their generous sharing of photographs and personal reflections have made this work possible. Special thanks should be given to Mr. and Mrs. Clarence Brodeur of New Haven, Connecticut, who gave generously in time, materials, and inspiration. Dr. Fiora Contino and Dr. J. Donald Robb are thanked for their fine ensemble of letters and notes from many years of association with Mademoiselle. Even those who refused to assist are thanked for bringing the diversity of her pervasiveness to my mind.

All materials have been traced as clearly as possible. Attempts have been made to clarify all copyright holders. There has been no intent to omit any acknowledgments. Many of the stories and comments made by Mademoiselle Boulanger were recorded by different sources. She, too, adjusted many stories for use in varied contexts. Any omissions will be clearly rectified in future printings.

Gertrude Stein made a rule early in this century:

You can be a museum or modern, but you cannot be both.

Nadia Boulanger was both. She was a woman in a man's world. She was a devout Christian in a century of complex questioning. These points bring abstract struggles to mind. All are not logically resolved by a paraphrase of a technique. But the power of great art hinges on the duality of these abstractions. Boulanger brought these to her students. It is that power and it alone that demands reflection.

Don G. Campbell

March 21, 1984
Dallas, Texas

Acknowledgments

ARCHIVES DE L'ACADEMIE DES BEAUX-ARTS IN PARIS
THE FONTAINEBLEAU MUNICIPAL ARCHIVES
THE NATIONAL ARCHIVES IN PARIS
THE ARCHIVES OF THE PALAIS OF MONACO
THE BRITISH LIBRARY IN LONDON
THE NATIONAL CONSERVATORY OF MUSIC IN PARIS
THE CRANE SCHOOL OF MUSIC ARCHIVES
THE FONTAINEBLEAU ALUMNI ASSOCIATION
THE LIBRARY OF CONGRESS IN WASHINGTON, D.C.
THE NEW YORK PUBLIC LIBRARY
NORTH TEXAS STATE UNIVERSITY MUSIC LIBRARY, THE HELEN HEWITT COLLECTION
THE AMERICAN ORGANIST MAGAZINE
STUDIO THÉO COLLECTION
RICE UNIVERSITY LIBRARY
THE HUMANITIES RESEARCH CENTER AT THE UNIVERSITY OF TEXAS
THE YALE MUSIC LIBRARY
THE ORAL HISTORY LIBRARY AT YALE
THE NEW YORK TIMES
THE HERALD TRIBUNE, PARIS EDITION
THE MUSIC MAGAZINE
THE PIANO QUARTERLY
LIFE MAGAZINE
TIME MAGAZINE
THE JAPAN TIMES
MRS. ENA WHITE
MS. SANDY BEYER

Grateful appreciation is extended to the countless friends, associates and students of Nadia Boulanger, who made this work possible, especially;

Clarence Brodeur
Marie Brodeur
Harriett Ely
J. Donald Robb
Annette Dieudonné
Paul Vellucci
Ada Nelson
Ann Gilmore
Annie Dubouloy Da Silva
Douglas Lyttle
Aaron Copland
Virgil Thomson
Ned Rorem
Louise Talma
Helen Hosmer
Leonie Rosenstiel
Flore Wend
Fiora Contino
Narcis Bonet
Emil Naoumoff
Fr. Edward McKenna
Mildred Campbell
Leonard Bernstein
Gaby Casadesus
Nicholas T. Brill
Elaine Brown
Giovanni Lelli
Hugh Mercer
Vivian Perlis
Albert Tessier
Marion Tournon-Branly
Ruth Bampton

Mary Helen Chapman
W. David Noakes
Diane Shattuck
John Ferrante
Perry Beach
Betty Blakeslee-Batt
Charles K. Agle
Barbara Shapiro Alexander
John Ardoin
Marianne Barouch
Antoine Battaini
Seymour Bernstein
Ethelston Chapman
Catherine Sloane Coffin
William Cooper
Marion Cooper
Larry Walz
Florence Sloan
Donald Harris
James S. Harrison
Walter H. Hodgson
Stephen F. Johnson
Gilberte LeCompte
Jocelyn Mackey
Don McAfee
John Price
Fred R. von der Mehden
Harriet Simons
Elsie Watson
Ralph Wakefield
Richard Forrest Woods
Gladys Burke

MASTER TEACHER

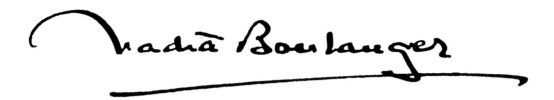

To measure the potency of Boulanger's influence is impossible. As a tree is rooted firmly to the earth, she was rooted in the history and grammar of Western music. She was gifted with genius, grew with unmatched stability and branched out to hundreds directly and to thousands in sympathetic manner.

She was nurtured by her students as she took their musical seeds and insisted on their growth. Her wisdom dominated their appetites for technique and fortitude.

Her lucid expression never wavered as age withdrew power from her physical being. She left an abundance of musical inspiration for all generations. This book is a remnant of her wisdom, musicianship, and power.

1968, Studio Théo.

2

Reflections

ON THE MASTER TEACHER

"So far as musical pedagogy is concerned —
    and by extension musical creation —
    she is the most influential person who ever lived."

NED ROREM
1979

With Fontainebleau students, 1958. Studio Théo.

"She was like a philosopher's stone which could transmute the musical souls of her students, purging them of the lesser and unpurified qualities of technical discipline."

DON G. CAMPBELL
1971

3

1963, Studio Théo.

"She was a one-woman graduate school, so powerful and so permeating that legend credits every United States town with two things: a five and dime and a Boulanger pupil."

VIRGIL THOMSON
1960

"The secret of her influence, many of her students say, is that she had no preconceived notions about teaching, music or life. She was interested in one thing: getting the most out of the pupil. To achieve this, she demanded discipline and integrity from the student. Her aim was to instill in the student a solid background, one which she considered the rock essentials. She herself belonged to no school of composition, no sect of musical thought, and she impatiently dismissed all the current 'isms' as tools."

HAROLD SCHONBERG
1958

"There are rare men and women whose prime function it is to bring us 'valuable news of the travelling gods' — news of those gods of the mind and spirit of the world who travel between their day and ours, little known to us until they are brought closer through the sympathy and insight and genius of those who themselves are touched with a kind of supermundane and re-creative wisdom. Mlle. Boulanger was one of these. Her mind had something of that rich power and that candent energy which made it possible for her sympathies and imagination, like those of a different artist in a different art, to move with ardor through all the passions and dearness of existence."

LAWRENCE GILMAN
1959

"As a young woman she had a kind of objective warmth. She had none of the aesthetic intensity of a Martha Graham nor the toughness of a Gertrude Stein. On the contrary, in those early days she possessed an almost old-fashioned womanliness, one that was quite unaware of its own charm. Her low-heeled shoes and long black skirts and pince-nez glasses contrasted strangely with her bright intelligence and lively temperament."

AARON COPLAND
1960

5

"Her love of music was contagious, the depth and sincerity of her feeling immediately apparent, and the clarity of her judgment swiftly and forcibly communicated.

"The leading impression of anyone with whom she came in contact was unquestionably one of inexhaustive creative energy. Her nature combined to a rare degree both masculine aggressiveness and womanly charm. But this energy was the dominant, the power which conditioned every phase of her broadly constructed life, gave her such unusual clairvoyance and encouraged other creative artists to identify themselves in her."

HERBERT ELWELL
1937

"No one could forget her mind of steel. In the group class, we might think that we were safely hidden behind some flowers as Mademoiselle reduced Stravinsky scores at the piano while we conducted. But then later, at the private lessons, she would say:

You conducted these pages better yesterday, but you missed your cue in measure ten and in measure twenty you should begin with a crescendo.

At her studio piano, 1975. Studio Théo.

1964, conducting at the Menuhin Festival in Gstaad (Wend, Papuet, Cuenod, and Ochoa are singing. Menuhin and Lysy are at left). Photo courtesy of Flore Wood.

"Music was her life and she made others feel that it was their life, too. Unassuming, understanding, demanding, her spirit will live in the hearts of all those with whom she came in contact. Few can leave such a legacy."

JOCELYN MACKEY
1981

7

1972, teaching a harmony class at her Fontainebleau Palace apartment. Photo © Douglas Lyttle

"Often during evening lessons, the two sons of her servant, Giovanni and Paolo, would come to Mademoiselle just before going to bed. She would test them on naming the notes she played on the piano in a way a parent would review the colors or the alphabet. But when they made a mistake, she would sternly pat their bottoms. Occasionally one would cry and quickly made miscellaneous guesses of RE, LA, MI, SOL and so forth, trying to find the correct answer. After the seemingly endless moments of their distress, she once declared:

If I did not think you could name them, I would put myself in prison.

JOHN PRICE
1979

Nadia Boulanger with her two godsons who lived in the Rue Ballu apartment, Giovanni and Paulo Lelli.

At a master class at Fontainebleau, 1959. Studio Théo.

"Whether she played or spoke, her hands, subtle and strong, acted in harmonic accent to the message."

DON G. CAMPBELL
1971

10

"Ni Commencement ni Fin . . ."

The last visit I had with Nadia was on her last birthday. I don't think she knew it was her birthday, since she was in a coma. But nature seemed to know it, providing for the occasion an unforgettably radiant September Sunday, with the intense blue of the cloudless sky competing in saturation with the rich greens of the Fontainebleau gardens. The air trembled.

Everything conspired to urge me on to Fontainebleau that day: my one free afternoon in a three-week working visit to Paris, the exhilarating weather, and the certain knowledge that it would be my last time with her. On the other hand, there were some strong contra-indicative warnings from her closest friends and guardians: Mademoiselle would be disturbed and exhausted by a visit; she could not speak, and in any event would not recognize me. *Tant pis:* I paid my visit as if compelled.

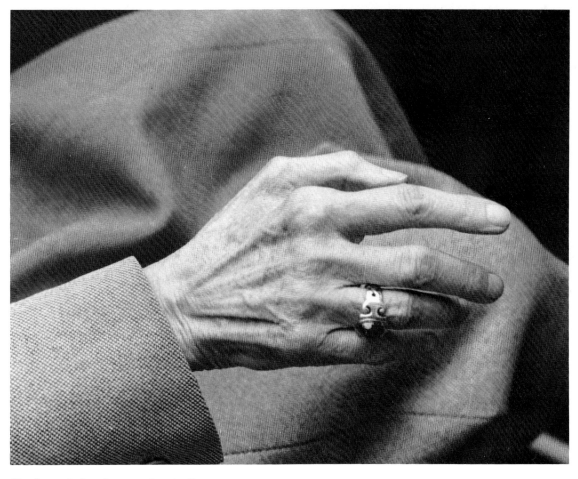

Boulanger's hand, 1977, by Guillermo Arizcoretta.

With Leonard Bernstein on her 90th birthday. To the right is Emil Nadumoff, her last protégé. Courtesy of Clarence Brodeur.

I was ushered into her bedchamber by the angelic and anxiety-ridden Mademoiselle Dieudonné, who, with forefinger to lips and seconded by an attending nurse, whispered a short order: *ten minutes only.* As it turned out, the visit lasted closer to one hour. Nadia was beautifully dressed and groomed, as if for the coffin. Her crucifix gleamed at her throat; her eyes and mouth were closed; her whole face seemed closed in coma. I knelt by the bed in silent communion. Suddenly there was the shock of her voice, deep and strong as always. (How? Her lips did not seem to move; how?)

Qui est la? (Who is there?)

I could not respond for shock. The Dieudonné forefinger whipped to the lips. Finally, I dared to speak: "Lenny. Léonard . . . ." Silence. Did she hear, did she know?

Cher Lenny . . . . .

She knew; a miracle. An encouraging signal from Dieudonné. I persevered: "My dear friend, how do you feel?" Pause. Then that basso profundo (through unmoving lips)

Tellement forte. (So far, strong)

I drew a deep breath. "Vous voulez dire . . . . interieurement?" (You mean inwardly?)

Oui . . . . mais le corps . . (Yes, but the body . . .)

"Je comprends bien" (I understand), I said hastily, to shorten her efforts. "Je pars. Vous devez être trés fatigué." (I'm leaving. You must be very tired.)

Pas de fatigué. Point . . . . (Not at all tired)

A protracted pause, and I realized she had drifted back into sleep.

Signals from the astonished attending ladies suggested my departure. I was held there, unable to rise from my knees. I knew there was more to come, and in a few minutes, it did come:

Ne partez pas. (Do not leave.)

Not a plea, but a command. I searched my mind anxiously for the right thing to say, knowing that anything would be wrong. Then I heard myself asking: "Vous entendez la musique dans la tete?" (Do you hear music in your head?) Her instant reply:

Tout le temps. Tout le temps. (All the time. All the time.)

This so encouraged me that I continued, as if in quotidian conversation: "Et qu'est-ce que vous entendez, ce moment-ci?" (Do you hear it now, at this moment?)
I thought of her preferred loves. "Mozart? Monteverdi? Bach, Stravinsky, Ravel?" Long pause.

Une musique . . . ni commencement ni fin . . . .

(A music . . . without beginning or end.)

She was already there, on the other side.

LEONARD BERNSTEIN

14

Life

OF THE MASTER TEACHER

Tracing the lineage of Nadia Boulanger takes us to the musical families of Saxony, the noble families of Russia and to the origins of Western music. Her heritage was steeped in the 19th century mannerisms of the Parisian theatre and music circles, the strict emotional nature of a Russian aristocrat, and a dual Catholicism, one of faith and one of music.

Within a month after the first French pianoforte was built by Érard, Frédéric Boulanger was born in 1778. Although the family lived temporarily in the city of Dresden in Saxony, they soon joined the Parisian world of arts where music flourished. He entered the National Conservatory at an early age and won the *First Prize* in Cello at the age of nineteen in 1797. He studied with the master cellist, Levasseur, and won a cello for his superior ability. His talent and interest extended to other musical arts. By 1816, he had joined the faculty of the Conservatory as a vocal coach. He was a musician in the King's Chapel and later became a professor at the Royal School of Music.

Frédéric Boulanger was the first of the family to receive a *First Prize* from the Conservatory. From his birth until the death of his granddaughter, Nadia, over two hundred years later, the name Boulanger made an important contribution to the musical world in France and around the world.

During Napolean's campaign in Russia, Frédéric Boulanger married a talented singer who had won the *First Prize* from the National Conservatory in 1809. Marie-Julie Hallinger was born January 29, 1786 near Paris. She grew up with a family that nurtured theatrical interests. After she received her *First Prize* in voice, she also received the same honor in Lyric Comedy. By 1812 she had made her debut and began her long career with the Opéra Comique in Paris.

Exactly seventy two years before the birth of Nadia Boulanger, her father was born to Marie-Julie Boulanger in Paris. Henri-Alexandre Ernest Boulanger was born on September 16, 1815. The rich aesthetic environment of his early life brought him in touch with the poets, writers, intellectuals, and musicians of the time. Marie-Julie's sister, Sophie, had married the foremost actor, Frédérich LeMaître, thus the family was part of the most prominent musical and theatrical circles. Ernest Boulanger attended the National Conservatory and by the age of twenty had received the *Grand Prix de Rome* for his work *Achille.* In 1836, he went to the Villa Medici in Rome to work and compose as his award. There were artists, painters, and musicians of varied sorts there as there would be for a century to come. It was the highest of honors for a young composer of his time. His stay was cursed by the cholera epidemic that forced the closing of the Villa. Although he was spared having the disease, he was forced to move to Florence with the other artists.

In the five years after his return from Italy, Monsieur Ernest Boulanger rose to fame in the Parisian world of music. His early operas *Le Diable á l'Ecole, Les Deux Bergers,* and *La Cachette* were all performed and well received by the middle of the century. He was close to his mother in these years. His father had died and he escorted his mother to all the musical and theatrical events. Soon after her retirement, she died of a ruptured blood vessel on July 22, 1850.

In the years that followed, he continued to write operas, large choral works and operettas. *Le 15 Aout au Champs, Les Sabots de la Marquise, Marion, L'Eventail, Don Quichotte* and *Don Muscarade* were all performed in Paris. He became a member of the jury for the *Prix de Rome,* which he had received himself.

It was not until he had been teaching at the National Conservatory and was fully mature and established, that Ernest became engaged. A very young Russian girl had come from St. Petersburg to study voice. She was of the nobility and insisted of her family that she be allowed to study music in Paris. Although she was only eighteen years of age, Ernest Boulanger asked Princess Raissa Mychetskaya to marry him. Permission was granted and they were married on his 62nd birthday in 1877 at the Chapel of the Regiment of Huntsmen of the Imperial Guard in St. Petersburg. They were blessed by the chaplain of the Guard and the arch-priest. Although she was Russian Orthodox, she became a Roman Catholic and never sought to reinstate her noble or orthodox ties.

Their wedding was exactly a decade before the birth of Nadia. The couple moved to an apartment near the Gare du Nord on Rue Maubeuge in Paris. Madame Boulanger had been well educated in languages and music and was able to fit graciously into the Boulanger tradition, which was already a century old.

Ernest Boulanger had received the honor of Knight of the Legion of Honor some years before their marriage. In 1881, he became an officer of the National Academy. Although he was respected, he was at times criticized by his contemporaries for writing over-simplified music with little contrast. Nadia later spoke of him as a good musician, who wrote music of his time, not of the

Marie-Julie Hallinger Boulanger, circa 1814. Painting from Nadia Boulanger's private collection.

Ernest Boulanger, circa 1840. Painting from Nadia Boulanger's private collection.

future. His friendships with Gounod, Massenet, and Saint-Saëns were lasting and essential to the professional quality of his life.

Princess Raissa Mychetskaya was born on December 19, 1858, in St. Petersburg. Her noble family can be traced back as far as 1246 to St. Mikahil Tchernigovsky. The family Mychetsky flourished in the Taroussa, later called the Kalouga, Moscow, and St. Petersburg regions. One branch of the family was known in Poland. There seems to be no trace of musicianship recorded in the family and, after the Russian Revolution, little contact remained with Raissa, who altered her name to the accepted French spelling of Mychetsky.

As a young child, Raya, as called by her parents, studied music and decided to devote her life to it. After a great deal of consternation, she was allowed to go to Paris to study voice. After attending a concert where Ernest Boulanger conducted, she enrolled to study voice with him. Nadia spoke of her mother in those years: "She was really an amateur, never being a part of the teaching or performing world, but she was a true artist. She could listen, see, and understand the nature of things. She married young in the atmosphere of the Russian world and was emphatic about what was proper, in a way more so than even the French."

Madame Raissa Boulanger completely absorbed the way of life in Paris. She refused to speak Russian in the home, honoring her husband's inability to speak the language. She became a devout Roman Catholic and a strict adherent to the social mores of the time.

Bust of Nadia Boulanger's father, Ernest, and signed photos of Paul Valéry and André Gide, at the Rue Ballu apartment.

Raissa Mychetsky Boulanger, Nadia's mother, circa 1879. Painting from Nadia Boulanger's private collection.

On January 16, 1885, the first child was born to the Boulangers. Nina Juliette Boulanger was named after her father's grandmother. She was a very weak child and died fifteen months later on April 16, 1886. Exactly seventeen months thereafter, on Rue Maubeuge, Juliette-Nadia was born. She was received in the special light of her father's 72nd birthday being celebrated on that same day, September 16, 1887. It was also the tenth anniversary of the Boulanger's wedding.

Paris was in its radiant overture to the twentieth century. The Eiffel Tower was commissioned and began construction that year. The Great Exposition of 1889 was preparing to celebrate a centennial of the French Revolution. France prepared to make monumental statements to the world in the arts, sciences, and architecture. The time and lineage were correct for a brilliant being to be born. Abroad, Queen Victoria was celebrating her Golden Jubilee, William the Second was soon to become the Emperor of Germany, and Russia was challenging its tradition of royalty before the last Czar, Nicholas the Second. Liszt had recently died and the world of European arts, sciences, and political structures were breaking out of the Romantic and Royal patterns.

Nadia at age 5. Photo courtesy of Annette Dieudonné.

Within twenty years, the whole of Western society would be changed by social, political and artistic causes, and wars.

The Boulanger child was familiarly called Nadia, the French derivative of "Nadejda," a Russian name meaning "hope." Music was the exclusive language of her home. It was her link with the world, rather than newspapers or politics. She did not have any great musical interest in the early years. She did not like music at all and found it annoying. Stories were told that her sensitive ears would cause her to hide under the piano and moan when she heard music. Her mother was often asked if the young child were ill. Her father was perplexed by this strange and unhappy whim.

Nadia admitted later that the extraordinary moment came when she was three years old. A fire siren was sounding outside the apartment. She immediately went to the piano and tried to find the same pitch. She found the pitch and so discovered music. She admitted that she never left music after that time. She began to think in notes, rather than in words. She had slightly weak eyes and chose to learn to read music before learning to read simple books.

A few years before Nadia Boulanger died, in 1979, she recounted a story about her fourth Christmas at 30 Rue La Bruyére, where the family had recently moved. Her mother had asked her to go downstairs to give their neighbor, Madame Delpuget, Christmas greetings. When Nadia arrived, her neighbor said, "You are so kind to come. Tell me, did you have a Merry Christmas? What was given to you?" After a prolonged moment of thought, Nadia replied, "A bear and a farm." Madame responded quite opened-eyed, "A farm? A true farm?" At that very instant, little Nadia recalled an actual farm and began to describe everything she saw on the farm.

The following day, Madame Boulanger asked her daughter about the story she had told their neighbor about the farm. There was never any teasing in the home, there were never deceptions and the small child was punished. Mademoiselle Boulanger recalled 85 years later, that she could still see that farm. She recalled that true farm with a white house, a variety of animals, and a barn. It developed and nearly became Versailles in her imagination. This story represented to her the reality of the imagination that was necessary to create true art.

Within two years, a sister was born to Nadia. On August 21, 1893, Marie-Juliette Olga (Lili) Boulanger was born at the apartment on Rue La Bruyère in the ninth *arrondissement* in the shadow of Montmartre, close to the Salon that would be so well known on Rue Ballu.

By the time Nadia went to Finland and St. Petersburg with her mother in 1895, at age eight, she could read all the clefs, transpose, and play quite well.

Her father had been her first teacher. She began to study harmony and her mother taught her to read with her first book, *Le General Dourakine*. She remembered making the early mistakes in reading by interchanging the *"U"* and *"V"* sounds. She mixed up the *"H"* and the *"N."* Once during a driving test in America, she made the same mistake on an eye chart.

Her mother was most exacting and overly strict, allowing Nadia no allowances while practicing. She was made to memorize and play with only a glance at the score. She was serious, intelligent, and had an uncannily precocious intuition that allowed her to guess nearly everything her earliest teachers, such as Guilmant, were to say. Nothing was ever repeated of a general or specific nature. It was the clear definition given to her as a child from her family that created her phenomenal attention and concentration. When Lili was three years old, she, too, was able to sing pitches correctly without the use of the piano. In that same year, 1896, Nadia began to study piano, cello, and organ, even though she could not reach the pedals. She entered the National Conservatory in the tradition of her ancestors on December 10, 1896, as a student of Solfège at the age of nine. Monsieur Boulanger was now over eighty years old and had a notable attachment to his youngest daughter. Lili was a sickly child, yet one with a magnetic attraction. The fair skin, angelic face and dark brown eyes often attracted attention. She shared a room with Nadia during those years.

When Lili was still young, Nadia recalls her father placing the small child in her arms and asking her to take care of her. He made her promise to look after her welfare. The experience was so profound that she spoke of it even in the last decade of her life. In 1898, another sister, Marie-Louise, was still-born. It was the first close awareness Nadia was to have with death.

Mademoiselle Boulanger had serious memories of her father. They had long talks about aesthetics, art, and music. She remembered going to the cemetery with her father to visit her grandmother's grave in Montmartre, where she and all her family would come to rest. It seemed of primordial importance to visit the shrine of his mother every week.

By the end of the century, the musical interests and score reading of young Nadia had developed so well that she was studying organ with Alexandre Guilmant, piano accompanying with Paul Vidal, and harmony with Auguste Chapuis. All were in agreement as to her exceptional musicianship.

In the spring of 1900, on Good Friday, Ernest Boulanger called his good friend, Theodore DuBois, to his apartment to give him the duty of the protective care of his wife and daughters. William van der Boijen was asked to be a legal guardian. The following day, April 14, 1900, Ernest Boulanger died dur-

Nadia Boulanger at age 17. Photo courtesy of Annette Dieudonné.

Boulanger and her fellow students at the Conservatoire, circa 1908. Photo courtesy of Annette Dieudonné.

ing a conversation with Nadia. After his death, the room where he died was closed and never reused by the family. The daughters then became more resolved in their musical campaigns and studies.

During the next eight years, Nadia was totally absorbed in her musical studies at the Conservatory. She came to know André Caplet, Alfredo Casella, Georges Enesco, Florent Schmitt, Raoul Laparra, and Maurice Ravel in these formative years. Even before her father's death, she had won the *First Prize* medal in Solfège. In 1903, she obtained the same award in harmony and, in July of 1904, set the remarkable record of obtaining three First Prizes within four days in composition, piano accompaniment, and organ. By the age of 16, she had obtained every *First Prize* in her studies.

The month after the exams, the Boulanger family went to Gargenville, a small village about fifty kilometers northwest of Paris near the Seine. They visited the home of Raoul Pugno and decided to buy the three houses nearby called *Les Maisonettes*. The family also became acquainted with the influential poet, Paul Valéry. The small village became an important summerplace for artists for many decades and remained in the family until Nadia Boulanger's death.

After graduation from the National Conservatory at the age of 16, Nadia began to take on her own students, most of whom were older. The sisters were more often independent at that time, lived in separate rooms, and led different types of lives. Raissa Boulanger spent every moment caring for her daughters, in the strictest emotional, intellectual, and musical fashion possible. It was decided to move into another apartment in Paris. In October 1904, they moved to 36 Rue Ballu, near Pugno's apartment, on a street named after Théodore Ballu, the architect of the nearby Trinité Church, where they were already parishioners.

By that time, Mademoiselle Boulanger was studying more intensely with André Gedalge and Gabriel Fauré. She had become the assistant organist on the great Cavaillé-Coll organ at the Madeleine Church.

The apartment was an instant haven for the creative circles of the time, especially with the architects, music critics, and a medical doctor as neighbors. In the fourth-floor apartment was installed a 14-rank pipe organ built by Arstide Cavaillé-Coll. It was there, in late 1904, that the salon that was to teach composers for most of the century came into being.

The brilliance and genius of Nadia Boulanger set off her youth. Few souls come to earth with such enthusiasm and inner direction. Even fewer devote an absolute lifetime of quickened devotion to an art. There is no exaggeration in pointing toward her eight decades of concentration in musical performance and teaching as exceptional. It was in these years, without any self-awareness

36 Rue Ballu, home of the Boulangers for nearly 65 years.

other than music and her family, that she began to penetrate the music world as the most influential woman in the history of musical pedagogy. Piano and beginning-harmony students began to study with her. Annette Dieudonné came as a young girl and became the closest companion, musical associate, and friend for the whole of Nadia Boulanger's life. Lili would seldom be near her sister while she was teaching, but often accompanied her to the Conservatory and would attend the advanced classes.

From 1905, the summers were spent in Gargenville. It was there in 1906 that Lili composed her first piece, *La Lettre de Mort, The Letter of Death*. She was only thirteen years old.

Nadia Boulanger was studying with total dedication with Vidal, Vierne, Guilmant, Fauré, and Widor. She prepared her major work, *Sirène*, for the Grand Prix of Rome competition in 1908, and was awarded the Second Grand Prize. In 1904, another woman, Hélène Fleury, had won the same honor. Mlle. Lucienne Heuvelmans, a sculptress, reached the finals the same year as Nadia. She later sculpted the bust of Lili that was placed in the Rue Ballu apartment. After the competition, a shift of attention toward teaching more

Nadia Boulanger and companions, circa 1908.

25

Lili and Nadia dressed as Alsace and Lorraine for a party circa 1910

Nadia and Lili, 1913. Courtesy of Annette Dieudonné.

26

students and inspiring her sister began to dominate Nadia's life. She began to perform, and often played with Raoul Pugno. He had been on her final jury and had been a close friend of the family for four years. They often worked on music projects together and prepared the composition, *Les Heures Claires.*

Through her teaching, Nadia became the main financial source for her family. Most of her students were young ladies, although she did take on brilliant children such as her first protégé, Jacques Dupont. In 1909 she was assistant to Henri Dallier's organ class. The only record of her teaching her sister was in 1911 for a few months. Nadia wrote of her sister at that time: "What does she seek? What inner world has she built? What doubts her curious mind? She is already marked with sadness and her fragile body."

On February 22, 1912, Lili made her musical debut at a soirée in the Rue Ballu salon with her own composition and also performed a short piano work. Short, stout, and bearded Raoul Pugno played, as did Claude Debussy. Lili was continuously musical, singing and improvising vocally when she was well. She was always fragile, *gentile* and naive in the purest sense. Fauré came and taught her his new songs, which she could easily memorize and sing with him, even at four and five years of age. Just after her eighth birthday, she played for the first time in public at a mass at Notre Dame in Trouville.

As she grew older, she became meticulous in her notebooks, letters, and studies. Every exercise was numbered and dated. In 1913, Lili Boulanger became a noted figure in the French musical world. She was awarded the *Prix Yvonne de Gouy d'Arsy, Prix LePaulle,* and the most prestigious *Grand Prix de Rome* for her remarkable *Faust et Hélène,* which was dedicated to her sister.

The jury was so moved by her work, that before it was finished, they declared her the recipient of the award. The following day, an interview with Lili from the periodical, *The Musical Leader,* reported the following conversation: "Lili, what are your plans?" She responded, "To work for myself. I shall not give any lessons." The interviewer continued, "But after your great triumph of last evening, you certainly have not been able to sleep." Lili said, "Oh, yes indeed. I dreamed, didn't I mother? I dreamed that I was a little child and was teaching my doll to play the piano." Her mother then responded, "You see, she is still only a child."

Later in 1913, Nadia and Lilli gave a Gala Concert together at the Théâtre Léon Poirier. The evening opened with a short lecture by Landormy, and continued with the music of both Nadia and Lili.

It was a united triumph, appreciated by the public and applauded with great enthusiasm. In the last months of 1913, Raoul Pugno requested that Nadia accompany him to Russia for a series of concerts. She had been working

Lili Boulanger at the Cavaillé-Coll organ in the Rue Ballu apartment in 1913.

on compositions with him and she felt him to be one of her closest friends and associates. His bronchial illness caused a week's delay in Berlin on their way. The dire winter and the long journey on an inadequately heated train weakened him, and he died on January 3, 1914, in Moscow, while he was with Nadia. She had to accompany his body back to Paris without funds or assistance from musicians in Russia. The emotional coldness of Rachmaninoff left a life-long resentment with Nadia to him and his music. Nadia had gotten the measles during the last part of the trip. When she returned home, Lili became exposed and suffered with the illness and became distraught as she was preparing to depart for the Villa Medici in Rome to compose, as her father had done seventy-two years earlier.

Nadia and Lili at the Rue Ballu apartment on the day of Lili's award, the Grand Prix de Rome, *in 1913. Courtesy of Annette Dieudonné.*

Because of her illness, her arrival in Rome was delayed a number of times. She stopped in Nice to meet with Maurice Maeterlinck and made an agreement to use his play, *La Princesse Maleine,* as a source for an opera libretto. Finally, at the end of March, Lili arrived in Rome with her mother. She was weak and ill. The months that followed were painful. She worked on the *24th Psalm* and the *129th Psalm*. She saw little of the city that surrounded her. By the end of June, Lili had returned to Paris, knowing that her health and life were limited. Her family and friends sought methods of healing through the doctors of the day. A variety of methods were used and Lili was able to continue her composing. During the first half of 1917, she completed a sketch of *La Princesse Maleine* and completed *Du Fond de L'Abîme* and the *Vielle Prière Bouddhique,* which were started in the previous year. Her works were being performed in Europe and America, but her power to continue her work began to fail. The last months of 1917 and the early part of 1918 gave little hope for Lili's survival. The dreadful war, the potent chill of that winter and the dark fate of death did not completely destroy her childlike fervor or talent. Just weeks before her death, Lili dictated to Nadia the music statement of faith and salvation for her last testament, *Pie Jesu.*

Lili Boulanger wrote music because it was her soul. It was an inaccessible language of the musical art, grown to mature proportions, far more advanced than any other language she could control. Her innocent and death-driven life, her genius struggling to share itself, her being of faith and her naiveté, were as important as her music. Lili was not haunted by death as Mahler was; she was a sister to it. Her music was not composed of fear, terror, or distress; it was made of simplicity and faith. Her deathbed wish for her sister, mother, and friends was printed on her funeral announcement. It simply states:

I offer to God my sufferings so that they may shower down on you as Joy.

Lili died on March 15, 1918, in Mezy, at the age of twenty-four.

Without doubt, Nadia's life was reinforced by her sister. It is not altogether correct to say that she was Lili's teacher and that at her death Nadia gave up composition and dedicated her life to Lili's memory. This overused romantic paraphrase is partially true, but to look at the world with greater scope shows even more reasons why Nadia Boulanger became the pedagogue of the century.

The themes of death and music surrounded her world. The deaths of her father, her friend Pugno, and her sister, were even more defined by the pain and destruction of the Great War. She saw herself in the critical light of the world itself and saw her concentration in music as a means to assist in the world's plight. Her mother was a stable factor in her work and life. Nadia often recalled a story which enforced the way she lived and taught.

"When I was a student at the Conservatory, my mother and I were walking home. I had taken some classes that seemed easy to me. I was first in the class. I asked my mother if she was satisfied with my work. She responded:

Well, well, that is very nice, but do you consider that you have done all that you could have done?

When I heard this 'All,' it completely penetrated me. I know after all my life that I have never done *all* that I could. Work . . . yes, very much. But *all?* No. I have never exhausted the possibility of my effort."

So in those early years, Nadia Boulanger began her goal toward the "all" of music and work. She completed the manuscript that she had started with Pugno, *La Ville Morte, The Dead City.* Before Lili had died, Nadia agreed to assist General Huntzinger in arranging music for the soldiers. She began to work on projects to write letters to soldiers and arranged a committee from the National Conservatory to form an organization for the French soldiers so they would be able to study music. Francis Casadesus later started a separate project for a small school in Chaumont in 1917 for musicians in the American Army.

During December 1918, Lili's *Faust et Hélène* was debuted by the New York Symphonic Society in Carnegie Hall. Walter Damrosch thought it to be an early masterpiece of modern music and sought out Nadia for more of her sister's compositions.

Nadia came of prominent age professionally by the end of 1921. She performed in concerts to raise money for the orphans of the war. Lili's *Pour Les Funérailles d'un Soldat* was transcribed for organ and became somewhat of a theme in the next decade of Nadia's concerts.

In 1920, she succeeded Paul Dukas as teacher of music history at the Ecole Normale. She was active in the French League of Women's Rights and performed to raise money for its cause. It was in the early twenties that she confessed to her teacher, Fauré, that she would give up composition. Toward the end of his life, she said to him, "If there is anything of which I am very sure, it is that my music is useless." She refused to be critical of others before being critical of herself. In 1924, after his death, she replaced him as organist at the Madeleine Church.

Walter Damrosch was in France in 1921 and asked her what she planned for the summer. She replied that she would be in Gargenville as usual. He insisted that she join him in Fontainebleau.

Damrosch became the organizer. Francis Casadesus was the first director. Nadia went to Fontainebleau and began to teach harmony with only the

The faculty and student body of the first session of the American Conservatory in Fontainebleau, 1921. The front row commencing with the 7th from left: Charles-Marie Widor, Mrs. James Montgomery Tuttle, Director Francis Casadesus, President Maurice Fragnaud, Nadia Boulanger, Paul Vidal, Isador Philipp, André Hekking, André Bloch, Motte La Croix and Robert Casadesus. Aaron Copland and Albert Tessier were among the students.

English equivalents of *bonjour* and *au revoir*. Her career was launched internationally. The economics were staggering because all were poor after the war, but the rich enthusiasm of the Americans brought a dramatic quickening of the musical pulse. American music had developed late because of its isolation. The young Americans who attended the first session in Fontainebleau in 1921, such as Aaron Copland, Albert Tessier and Melville Smith, were exposed to a phenomenal faculty consisting of Paul Vidal, Charles-Marie Widor, Isidor Phillipp, Robert Casadesus, André Hekking, André Bloch, and Nadia Boulanger.

Copland recalls his first encounter with Mademoiselle: "I did not go to Paris to study with Nadia Boulanger and I really was not her first American pupil. I simply read an advertisement in *Musical America* that there would be a summer school for musicians in France. I would have not gone to France alone, but knowing that there would be other Americans there, I went. I was the first to enroll and was eager to study composition. I had no interest in studying harmony, having already completed its necessary requirements. But I went to her class. I expected an elderly lady reconstituting the harmonic laws of the past, but I found a brilliant young woman analyzing *Boris Godunov* by Modeste Moussorgski. I was impressed. I needed a teacher in Paris for the year, but was uncertain that I should study with a woman. No composer had ever studied with a lady. But I bravely asked her for lessons. I was not afraid of her, but of my reputation. The fear soon stopped. She took me to the basics of all music. She never made me go back. She only took me forward. She commanded everything, she ignited everything."

Copland and Boulanger enriched each other. He encouraged other American musicians to study with her; she encouraged him to write. She brought him to the attention of the musical public in America. Damrosch asked her to plan a trip to America in early 1925. He wanted her to have a special organ symphony composed for her to perform in New York.

She asked Copland to compose it. He was completely shocked. He knew nothing of the instrument and had never heard a note of his own orchestration performed, much less by a major orchestra. He was introduced as a composer in America through his French female teacher.

The twenties in Paris became a center for experimentation and abstraction. On the slopes of Montmartre lived Milhaud, Honegger, Gertrude Stein, and Erik Satie. Louis Durey, Georges Auric, Francis Poulenc, Jean Cocteau, and Germaine Taillefer were centered in the musical life of the city. Olivier Messiaen was organist at Boulanger's parish church, the Trinité. Tristan Tarza had made the declarations of Dada. The paintings of Marcel Duchamp, Max Ernst, and Pablo Picasso captured the daring visuals of the time. Stravinsky's *Firebird, Petrushka,* and *Rite of Spring* were coming to be a decade old. James Joyce was discussing the work of Ezra Pound. Roger Ducasse had dedicated his organ *Pastorale* to Nadia Boulanger.

The spring before the first session at Fontainebleau, Melville Smith had discovered Nadia. No matter what kinds of reforms were being made in the art circles of Paris, Nadia knew of them and constantly insisted on the perfection of the musical vocabulary of the past as assurance for freedom in the artist's future. Smith convinced Virgil Thomson that Nadia was the essential teacher for an American from Harvard. So in October, 1921, Smith, Thomson, and Hessenberg became her organ class. Copland had just started his private study with her. In the following years, Walter Piston, Herbert Elwell, Theodore Chanler, and George Antheil became early members of the "Boulangerie."

Palais de Fontainebleau — Conservatoire Américain
Boudoir des Laques   *Boudoir des Laques*
(Salon de réception)   (Reception room)
M. Francis Casadesus recevant   M. Francis Casadesus receiving
des journalistes Américains.   the american journalists.

(1) M. Francis Casadesus

Palais de Fontainebleau — Conservatoire Américain
La Classe d'Orgue   *The Organ class*
Professeurs : MM. Widor et Libert | Professors : MM. Ch. Widor et H. Libert
(1) M. Widor   (2) M. Francis Casadesus   (3) M. Fragnaud   (4) M. Libert

Postcards from the first year of the American Conservatory in Fontainebleau, 1921.

34

Palais de Fontainebleau — Conservatoire Américain
Classe de Chefs d'Orchestre   *Conducting class*
(1) M. Francis Casadesus   Professeur : M. Francis Casadesus | Professor : M. Francis Casadesus

(1) M. Robert Casadesus (fils)

Palais de Fontainebleau — Conservatoire Américain
Classe de Piano (Dir. : I. Philipp)   *Piano class* (Dir. : I. Philipp)
Professeur : M. Robert Casadesus (fils)   Professor : M. Robert Casadesus

35

Palais de Fontainebleau — Conservatoire Américain
Classe de Composition   *Composition class*
Professeur : M. Paul Vidal | Professor : M. Paul Vidal

(1) M. Paul Vidal

Serge Koussevitzky was vitalizing Paris with his remarkable series of concerts, which led him later to become conductor of the Boston Symphony Orchestra.

The Americans returned to the United States and began to speak of Boulanger, and to arrange and perform the music of Lili. Out of friendship for Boulanger, Thomson conducted a performance of *Pour Les Funérailles d'un Soldat* for the Harvard Musical Club. Later, he arranged the *Vielle Prière Bouddhique* for the Harvard Glee Club.

Thomson recalls the performance of the Copland *Organ Symphony*. When Boulanger asked him how he liked it, he replied that he had wept. "But the important thing is why you wept." He responded that he had wept because he had not written it himself. It was a Boulanger piece, it was an American piece and he was overjoyed that it had been written. Joy had also been in his tears.

Her American tour was highly successful. Copland's debut had caused an outcry by the conductor, Walter Damrosch, in New York. Immediately after its performance, he turned to the audience and said, "If a young man, at the age of twenty-three, can write a symphony like that, in five years he will be ready to commit murder!" Nadia Boulanger made no adjustment in her favorable attitude toward either the composer or the conductor of the performance.

Nadia Boulanger at the Grand Court Organ, John Wanamaker, Philadelphia, 1925.

Boulanger's 1924 harmony class at Fontainebleau.

In these important years, she was not shy about writing. She had become
music critic for *Le Monde Musical* in Paris. Rice Institute in Houston, Texas,
published her musical view of the times on Modern Music, the Debussy
Preludes, and Stravinsky, in the spring of 1926 after her visit to the Institute in
January of 1925. Rice University has generously allowed these early writings to
be reprinted in another section of this book.

Nadia knew well what had been developing in Vienna and in the German
world of music. Much of it amused her, but did not qualify for her standard of
beauty and expression. She seldom condemned, but clearly made her views
apparent.

Toward the end of the twenties, Roy Harris came to study with
Boulanger. He moved to the area of Gargenville to get away from people and
the city, to work on finding his own style. Mademoiselle was quite fond of
him, his Oklahoma accent, and his western and masculine manners. He gave
her driving lessons. Generations of students and friends found her to be a
complete contradiction to attentiveness on the road. Her control at the
keyboard had no link to the steering wheel.

Boulanger's later reputation of teaching into the night and with endless
obsession during the day was not as prominent in the late 1920's and early
1930's. There was time for many concerts, many conversations with the in-

tellectuals, writers, poets and, naturally, musicians of the time. Her friendship with Paul Valéry seemed essential to her own development. He was a true intellectual, and was known as a poet. She had known him and his wife since 1904 when her home was bought in Gargenville. Extensive conversations and letters were exchanged. He had worked closely with Gide and Stravinsky. Madame Valéry had studied piano with Nadia in the early years and their bonds of mutual intellectual discovery never ceased. This was a time when reading was important. Boulanger had covered the major works of philosophers, although she felt she knew little. Her Catholicism was paramount, although it never constricted her aesthetic freedom. Attending morning mass was a necessity for her, yet her devotion to all of music and her students was the primary focus of her life.

In 1945, she became professor of accompaniment at the National Conservatory, a title that remained constant until her retirement from that position in the late 1960's. At the Ecole Normale, she was professor of organ, harmony, counterpoint, and fugue. At her Rue Ballu apartment, she taught all branches of music. It was not a detached or separate study. It was simply a necessity to know everything.

By the 1930's, the apartment on Rue Ballu was an established axis in the music world. Its turn-of-the-century furnishings were to have little alteration

The 1926 composition class at the Fontainebleau Palace.

Nadia, 1932.

for the coming fifty-five years of work. The Cavaillé-Coll organ took its prominent place along with two grand pianos, an Erard and a Steinway. It was a parlor museum of art, portraits, books, manuscripts, and mementos of her father and sister. There were cherished photos and gifts from Fauré, Gide, Debussy, Stravinsky, and Saint-Saëns. In the future decades, works and autographs of Marc Chagall, Paul Valéry, Francis Jammes, Georges Rouault, Renoir, and de St. Exupéry were added. The most modern scores and the rarest madrigals filled the shelves throughout the rooms. The Wednesday afternoon classes varied from Bach cantatas, Beethoven quartets, and Gesualdo experiments, to Mahler and Schönberg songs. Nothing was predictable except the growth of the musical mechanisms of the selected students.

At the end of these sessions, Mademoiselle Boulanger's aged mother would serve tea and sweet little cakes. She seldom said much, but was a presence, seemingly happy and clearly aware of her daughter's importance. Copland recalled how verbal Madame Boulanger was in his first years in Paris, saying things to her daughter in a genuinely shocking manner.

Madame Raissa Mychetskaya died on March 19, 1935. This woman is to be respected for the power and influence her daughter had on students and associates. Nadia recalled, "I had many teachers, professors, but my judge, my mentor, was my mother. She had the courage to make me learn. She observed everything. She came to my lessons and recorded everything. She dominated my growth and my ability to pay attention. She was undeniably intelligent and she adored me. In other places life passes and it is forgotten, but not in our home. This development for me was possible."

Mlle. Boulanger remembered two statements her mother made that had lasting impact on her. "Nadia, please do not, above all, embrace me every day at the same time. That would make it a habit." "Do not forget that your days are blessed, whether you see their gifts or not, they are blessed."

By the late 1930's, Mademoiselle, as she would be called throughout her life, had become recognized in large and prominent music worlds. Not only had she assumed the position of a musician's musician, but also achieved an image of respect that no other woman had realized. She had met the Princess Jean de Polignac and was invited to prepare a series of concerts for the elite patrons of the art. It was common to hear of Boulanger's chamber concerts of vocal and instrumental music at the Hotel George V and the Interallied Club in central Paris. Her audiences not only included the patrons, scholars, and musicians of the time, but also children. She had instituted the first series of children's concerts at the Ecole Normale early in that decade.

Mademoiselle had always been interested in early music, in the masterworks of musicians unknown to the public. It was with a small group of singers that she read, rehearsed, and performed works by Monteverdi, Schutz, Bach, and Carissimi, that had been dormant for centuries. By 1938, her small ensemble was made up of Doda Conrad, Hugues Cuénod, Nathalie and Irene Kedroff, Gisele Peyron, and the Contesse de Polignac. A series of broadcasts brought the music of this group to public attention in Poland and England. Fortunately, there are recordings of early Monteverdi madrigals made during those years. Mademoiselle did not claim to have rediscovered them herself since she was aware of the work Charles Bordes and Vincent D'Indy had done with the same early music. Yet, she did bring Monteverdi and a vast amount of early music to the conscious mind of musicians and audiences throughout Europe.

In November 1936, Boulanger conducted the Schutz *Histoire de La Résurrection* and premiered the Fauré *Requiem* in London. The following year she became the first woman to conduct the Royal Philharmonic in London.

Her second trip to America was commissioned by the French as a study in the pedagogy of music in American colleges and universities. During this time, Stravinsky had become ill in Paris and asked Boulanger to conduct the premiere of his commissioned work, *The Dumbarton Oaks Concerto,* in Washington, D.C. Thus, on May 8, 1938, she was instated as an important and distinguished musician in America. Serge Koussevitzky invited her to conduct the Boston Symphony Orchestra in February 1938. Moses Smith reviewed that concert:

> *She probably became the first woman to ever conduct a major symphony orchestra. She is as self-effacing as she is efficient as musician. She sees, according to repeated expression, no reason for personal glorification of the performer in music. And she has been perhaps even more insistent that the accident of her sex has nothing whatever to do with her conducting.*
>
> *The modest little woman in an inconspicuous black dress, thus occupied ironically the center of the stage even when she was seated far off to one side before the organ console that does considerable duty in Copland's Symphony.*
>
> *She seemed to be neither underscoring nor understating, but rather, to be releasing perfectly natural expression.*

By mid-February of the following year, 1939, she had become the first woman to conduct the New York Philharmonic and the Philadelphia Orchestras. Many invitations followed in the years ahead to visit colleges, universities and orchestras throughout the country. On March 6, 1939, the inaugural concert for the Lili Boulanger Memorial Fund was held in Boston. Mademoiselle Boulanger conducted *Psalm 130 (Du Fond de l'Abîme), Pour les Funérailles d'un Soldat,* and the solemn *Pie Jesu.* E. Power Biggs was organist.

At the same time, she was doing extensive teaching of harmony, counterpoint, composition, and performance at Radcliffe, Juilliard, Wellesley College, and at the Longy School of Music in Cambridge, Massachusetts. Barbara Trask and Winifred Johnstone assisted with the secretarial and organizational needs for the great demands put on Mademoiselle during that time and for the awesome war years soon to come.

Her former student, Herbert Elwell, summed up her influence in a short program commentary:

> *If there is any explanation for the breadth of her sympathies and imaginative scope, it is perhaps that she is efficiently operative both as a human being and as an artist. With her dynamic vitality, she generates a current that constantly seeks and uncovers in music whatever is alive and translatable in terms of human experience.*

42

Nadia Boulanger, 1937. Photo courtesy Harriet Ely.

Her student list had already become impressive. In the '20's she had influenced Copland, Thomson, Carter, Elwell, and Chandler. As children, Jean
Françaix and Yehudi Menuhin had become students. Douglas Moore spent a
season in 1920 studying organ with her. Roy Harris, Walter Piston, Roger Sessions, and Melville Smith were familiar on Rue Ballu. The '30's brought scores
of other students to her: Marc Blitzstein, David Diamond, Peggy Granville-
Hicks, Irving Fine, Elie Siegmeister, Louise Talma, Arthur Berger, and Robert
Russell Bennett. Not all were Americans. Ruth Slenczynska, Israel Citkowitz,
and Alexei Haieff were students at the time. There were dozens more from
many backgrounds. The American Conservatory in Fontainebleau was becoming an important bridge between American musicians and the French
interpretation of piano, organ, and string music. Boulanger had made many
friends in America by the early 1940's. By that time, growing interest and sup-
port was coming throughout the United States for this unique, English speaking Conservatory. Robert Casadesus, Igor Stravinsky, and Walter Damrosch all
served on the faculty. A Fine Arts faculty for students of painting, sculpture,
and architecture had been developed and attracted other young, talented
Americans.

Yet, by 1940, the imposing war was a threat to the school and the complete way of life in France. It was resolved to continue the school in 1940 under
the most austere circumstances. Nadia Boulanger had begun a war relief fund
through the Fontainebleau Alumni Association in the United States. The hundreds of dollars that were raised were used to assist musicians who were suffering from the war. Mrs. Robert Woods Bliss, from her home at Dumbarton
Oaks in Washington, D.C., became the chairperson. Before the May 10 in-
vasion, Mademoiselle wrote to her friends in America:

*How can I express my thanks! Be sure to tell all what my gratitude is.
Every contribution facilitates an undertaking which is most difficult. I
live in such admiration of the miracles of heroism we witness each day
that I no longer know which dominates . . . pity, horror or splendor.*

*There is so much to be done to render bearable the intolerable pa-
tience demanded of these millions of men. The morale of the boys, of
the men who have abandoned everything to do their duty is in-
describable, their strength, courage and good humor. So much greatness resulting from such a horror! And so to pray, to hope and in this
obscurity, to wait, to learn patience and to smile, so that life may find
light from the serenity of the heart. Difficult.*

*I conducted the other day an orchestra of soldiers at the front. You
can't imagine, all those men in uniform, some of them just coming*

44

The Louis IX wing of the Fontainebleau Palace, which housed the American Conservatory from 1921 until 1979.

The 1962 class on the horseshoe steps of the Fontainebleau Palace.

Boulanger and Stravinsky, 1941. Photo courtesy of the Gilmore Collection.

down from the front lines and such an atmosphere of religious atten-
tion: Mozart, Bach and would you believe? Debussy's 'Dieu, qu'il la
fait bon regarder' was heard in complete silence.

On March 14, 1940, Igor Stravinsky conducted a concert of his music at
Town Hall in New York to raise money for Boulanger's relief fund.

Friends like Marie and Clarence Brodeur in America and Ethel Thurston
in France gave of themselves for the needs of the war. The French troops had

already taken over the country near Mademoiselle's home in Gargenville and Paris. She made constant shuttles in her car carrying people to Brittany. Gossip spread in America that she was driving an ambulance.

By the first of November 1940, Nadia Boulanger had arrived in the United States. It was not a simple decision for her to leave her country during the war years. Her affections, musical friendships and purposes in America were clear, but that noble sense of nationalism always dominated her political and social responsibilities. She had planned to teach in Cambridge, Massachusetts in September, but due to the enormous complications in travel and passport control, she was two months late. Her energy for raising funds through the arts never ceased throughout the war. She conducted a program of Fauré and Schutz with the New York Philharmonic and the able assistance of Helen Hosmer and the Potsdam State-Crane Choir. This benefit, on April 4, 1941, at Carnegie Hall honored the recently deceased Jan Paderewski and supported the Polish exiles in Great Britain and Switzerland.

Many concerts followed for the French Relief Fund. Mademoiselle traveled throughout the country accepting lecture series, concerts, and private students for short and extended studies. She was invited by Milhaud and Stravinsky, then in California, to speak at Mills College in Oakland. She came to know Washington and Baltimore and the most active musicians and teachers in the country. There was always a curious and devoted interest in her, yet there were those who did not agree with her methods, but respected her manners. There were schools of new music who criticized her conventionalism and technical disciplines. These were but minor themes and ones that were completely offset by her brilliant command of the musical language. She was at home with music and the place was of much less importance. She taught Gabrielli to the school children at the Avon Old Farms school in Connecticut. She knew the conductors of the major orchestras she conducted and spoke with them about new music, American music: Koussevitzky in Boston, Gabrilowitasch in Detroit, Stock in Chicago, Stokowski in Philadelphia, and Damrosch in New York. She even appeared as a guest on Benny Goodman's radio program before she returned to France at the end of the war. She commented at that time on American music's uniqueness:

I see that American composers are distinguished by their marked feeling for rhythm, for the element of composition in their works and for the cultivation of their individuality. Their works show a direct power in handling the element of form. The American type of music is not founded on jazz, as is often said, it is simply to be known that jazz is truly American.

The faculty and harmony students at Fontainebleau, 1954. Studio Théo.

Her last series of major concerts during the war years in America consisted of the debut of Stravinsky's *Sonata For Two Pianos,* which she and Richard Johnson played in Wisconsin. She prepared programs of Fauré's music with the Harvard Glee Club, the Radcliffe Choral Society, and the Boston Symphony Orchestra. Her imprint had been indelibly made on Americans and their music.

By mid-1946, Mademoiselle Boulanger had returned to France and the tradition of lessons and classes on Rue Ballu and at the Conservatory was reinstated. The Conservatory at Fontainebleau was able to reopen through the financial assistance of Isabelle Kemp and a large number of donations from the Alumni Association. The hard-working committee was headed by Gerald Reynolds, and enormous assistance was received from Mr. and Mrs. Clarence Brodeur, Charles DuBose and Natalie Tuttle Martin. Robert Casadesus was director and reported to the American alumni that ten piano students had enrolled that year.

For Nadia, March 15 still marked a day of absolute devotion to both Lili and her mother. A memorial mass was offered in the Trinité Church with Lili's music being performed. No lesson was ever taught on that day and no casual entertaining was done. In 1948, a special concert of Lili's music was arranged in the Salle Gaveau. Nadia's pledge to her father to attend to the welfare of her sister was still in effect.

Olivier Messiaen had been appointed Professor of Composition at the Paris Conservatory while Nadia was in America. She long regretted that she was not there during that appointment, so that she might have been considered for it. Jacqueline Holingue became the first secretary to Mademoiselle immediately after the war. There were hundreds upon hundreds of scores and manuscripts for filing and labeling. Paris was still in dreadful condition after the war, with little food and sparse heating. It was then that a diary was kept of the daily duties or responsibilities. It was the mode of communication for the household. In 1948, Margherita and Guiseppi Lelli entered the household to cook and attend to the apartment.

Fontainebleau faculty: LeCompte, Pillois, Martinelli, Boulanger in 1956. Bernac and Poulenc are standing in the rear. Studio Théo.

Correspondence was very important to Nadia Boulanger. She wrote thousands of notes, cards, and letters each year. She remembered anniversaries of life and death. She announced congratulations and condolences. On her sixtieth birthday in Paris, she was given a treasured gift by her one most respected living composer, Igor Stravinsky. He composed the *Petit Canon Pour La Fête de Nadia Boulanger* for two tenors with the text by Jean de Meung. Other such musical gifts were often to come during the next three decades. She later spoke of Stravinsky with utmost respect:

> *Who is he? He was a power that no dictionary could define and of which you can find no explanation. What is his personality? It was his style, as a master. It dominated him before he needed to use it.*

Rue Ballu again was alive in its total musical body. Aspiring young students were hardly amazed to see Artur Rubenstein, Yehudi Menuhin, Sir Clifford Curzon, Charles Munch, or Sir John Barbirolli as guests. Within the large double doors, time somehow stopped. The interior had been just as comfortable and curious to Erik Satie, Béla Bartók or Stravinsky during the previous generation. The room had small paintings, icons, silver letter openers, Chinese vases, and hundreds of memorabilia. Each object had its own timbre and story. It was a collage of little gifts and precious art. In its own way the room was cluttered with a charmed warmth. It was a statement that the two previous centuries would never completely die. There were no threats of electronic sounds of synthesized tonality, except for her phonograph. It was a *déjà vu* and a new experience all at once. It is fortunate that these main rooms are being reconstructed by the National Conservatory and the National Library in Paris.

The thousands of books, manuscripts, and notes were in meticulous order. Documents were classified and all the music was covered in brown paper. Mademoiselle Boulanger never marked in them, even where there were mistakes. Somehow the printed page was sacred, whether it was written by Monteverdi or Françaix.

Her days and years were organized for the '50's and '60's. Her classes at the Conservatory were held on Mondays and Thursdays in piano accompaniment. Monday afternoons were spent in correspondence. The first Monday of the month she would direct a concert for the Interallied Club. On Wednesday afternoons, she gave her analysis class in the apartment and would serve tea and receive guests. She had over thirty godchildren and they would all be invited for her Christmas Tree party. She was passionate and excessive, clear and focused, generous and demanding.

Students would wait in the small ante-chamber of the fourth-floor apartment on Rue Ballu. They were not allowed to use the ancient, art deco elevator. As they waited, it was easy to hear her sing with the syllables of *"tah, tah, ti, ti, tah, pi, pi, tah, tah, tah."* Then the solfèged syllables would take their place. Every lesson was exact and formal. No money was ever given to her directly as payment. It was left in an envelope in the other room or near the flowers on a table. Formality was distinct and natural.

The student roll continued to grow: Marcelle de Maziarly, David Ward Steinman, Daniel Baremboim, Piere Petit, Phillip Glass, Ruth Robbin, Idil Beret, Julia Perry, Roger Matton, Lennox Berkeley, Thea Musgrave, and Quincy Jones. Even Joe Raposi, musical creator of the Muppets, studied with her. By the 1970's, there were Asians, South Americans, and Eastern Europeans coming to Fontainebleau and Rue Ballu. Mario di Bonaventura, Luise Vosgerchian, and Narcis Bonet became students and admired friends for the rest of her life. She visited the world, but never as a tourist. She admitted to only an hour in Greece, an hour at the Hermitage in St. Petersburg and an hour in the museums of Madrid, Venice, and London. She told of the distress of having only an hour, but during that hour, the reality was endless and actually more than a clocked hour because to her the impression and the memory were there forever.

Many lessons took the same form, although nothing was predictable except work, results, and growth, whether they be painful or pleasurable. In a composition lesson, the student sat in a chair to her right as she sat at the piano. She would read the student's work silently and then play it quite perfectly without saying a word. Then comments would begin to flow as the music was diagnosed.

The summer sessions at Fontainebleau florished. Lucie Delacluse had been a devoted administrator for decades. The Ballu apartment virtually moved its personality to Fontainebleau each summer. With the high ceilings, grand mirrors, and view of the elegant gardens, Nadia truly had inherited a regal palace. The room was filled with photos, prized gifts, paintings, sculpture, and Tasha, the beloved cat. The light and space gave greater dimensions to each object. The faculty was outstanding: Jean and Robert Casadesus, Jean Pasquier, Annette Dieudonné, Mme. Gautier-Léon, Germaine Martinelli, Gilberte LeCompte and the unforgettable French teacher, Marthe Pillois. Rubenstein, Curzon, Menuhin, Marchal, Dupré, Souzay, and hosts of others gave master classes. Poulenc, Bernac, and guests from Poland and Hungary shared in the classes and concerts.

By the late 1950's, Nadia Boulanger was seventy years old. Suddenly, the world began to pay tribute. She was not older; her spirit seemed younger. Her

The faculty and students at Fontainebleau, 1955. Studio Théo.

mind was clear and continuing to grow and incorporate musical experimentations. She respected Zoltan Kodaly's musical system. She highly acknowledged the Eurhythmic work of Emile Jaques-Dalcroze, yet did not incorporate movement into her own pedagogical procedures. She had no interest in the Orff Schulwerk because she no longer had any interest in teaching general music in any type of public institution. The momentum continued without deviation from the intensity of her life.

A biographical sketch thus becomes suspended, just as time evaporates for an artist absorbed in the creative act. Data become a lengthy role of impressive moments: the 1954 Scandinavian tour, the 1956 visit to Warsaw as a judge in the International Festival for Contemporary Music, and the 1966 in-

52

vitation to Moscow as a member of the jury for the Tchaikovsky competition. Her student lists became directories. Her reflections were captured by thousands as she was invited by the Institute of Contemporary Arts in Washington, D.C. as a visiting artist and professor in 1958.

Her aura was delightfully captured by a film made by NBC for its Wisdom series. Her recordings of Monteverdi, Charpentier's *Medée*, operatic excerpts of Jean Philippe Rameau and a host of selections from the vocal music of the French Renaissance were released by Decca records. She was the Master of the Chapel of the Palace in Monaco and had selected the music and conducted the Stravinsky *Mass* for the wedding of Prince Rainier III and Princess Grace in 1956.

She revisited the United States in 1962, recelebrating the musical depth of Fauré's *Requiem* with the New York Philharmonic. There were scores of other engagements and interviews seeking her statements about music. Once in Washington, when asked a question about the origins of contemporary music, she simply started to name in strict chronological order without any notes, as usual, over seventy five compositions from Fauré to Messiaen. The years brought honors. There were numerous doctoral degrees, including distinguished honors from Harvard, Oxford, and Yale. She was invited to the White House as a dinner guest of President and Mrs. John F. Kennedy in 1962. The tributes brought appreciation from her, but did not detract from her ceaseless rigor in preparing the framework for beauty so that her students could come to fulfill their own destiny in art.

Whether she was conducting a concert at the Bath Festival or giving a class to children at Menhuin's school in England, she was the same. Students would return to Fontainebleau, including some who had retired from their

Poulenc's greeting for Nadia's 70th birthday in 1967.

36 RUE BALLU
PARIS IXE

TEL. TRI. 57-91

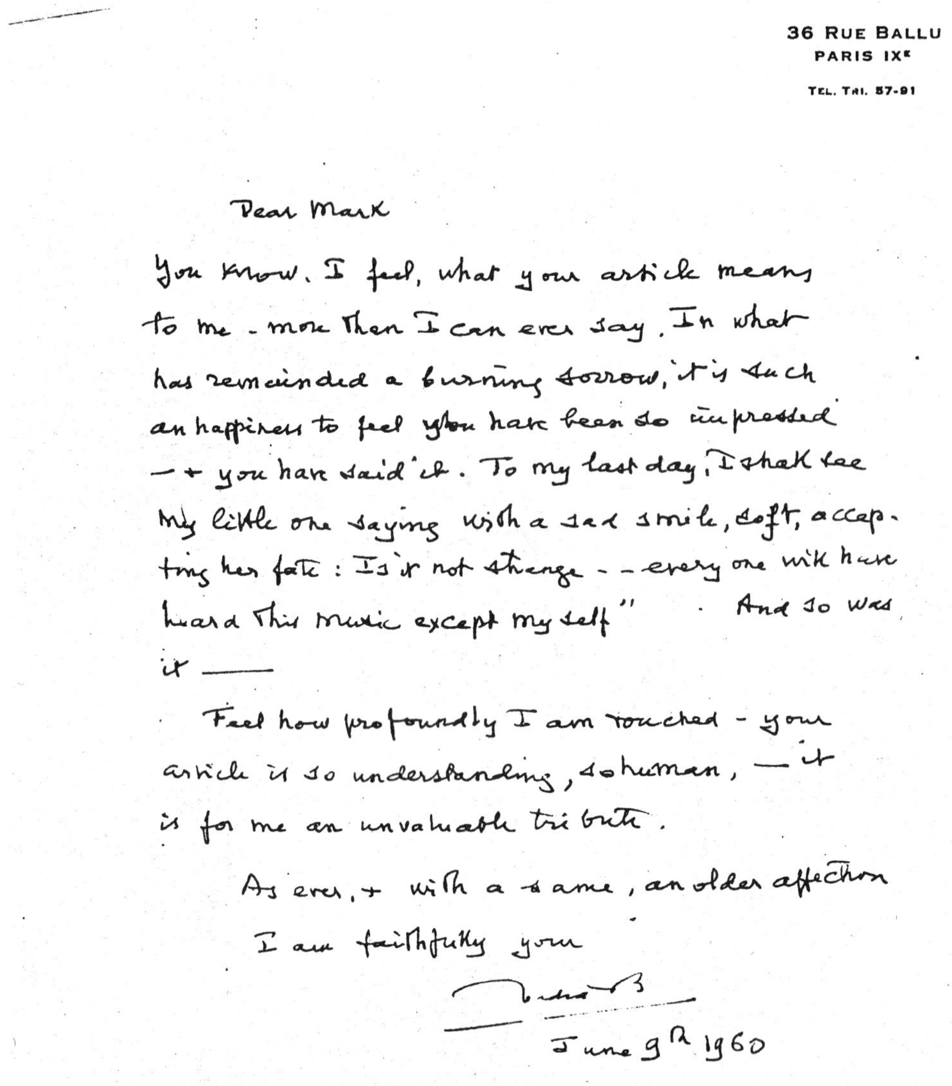

Dear Mark

You know, I feel, what your article means to me - more than I can ever say. In what has remainded a burning sorrow, it is such an happiness to feel you have been so impressed — + you have said it. To my last day, I shall see my little one saying with a sad smile, soft, accepting her fate: "Is it not strange - - every one will have heard this music except my self". And so was it ——

Feel how profoundly I am touched - your article is so understanding, so human, — it is for me an unvaluable tribute.

As ever, + with a same, an older affection

I am faithfully your

Nadia B

June 9th 1960

Boulanger's 1960 letter to Marc Blitzstein in regard to his article on Lili.

own college teaching careers and had initiated studies with Mademoiselle in the 1920's. Diana Ferenczfy and Annette Dieudonné were trusted assistants. The Lelli family still provided assistance in the Paris apartment.

Another anniversary for another decade of devotion had come. Mademoiselle was 80 years old in September 1967. Prince Rainier III asked Igor Markevitch to plan and direct a birthday celebration for her. Her closest friends and associates were invited from all over the world and truly reflected the royalty itself among musicians, educators, artists, and poets.

She adored the parties and while demanding none of the attention strictly observed during lessons, her presence was singularly brilliant. She sat with politicians, ambassadors, actors and children. She could find as much interest in Jackie Stewart, the auto racer, as she could in Richard Burton, the actor, or an anonymous child. In one of her last recorded interviews for the Yale University Oral History project, she recalled this brief story to Vivian Perlis:

You can see personality, you see it in a baby. Even in a baby of two months, the way it knows to smell, to look and to move. One day I received the niece of one of my pupils. She was two and a half years old. The lovely little girl had lovely little shoes, little leather shoes. And I said, "What lovely shoes! I love them so much." She began to weep bitterly. I said, "What have I said with my broken English, that she did not understand?" And her answer to me while still weeping was just that "They are too small. I cannot give them to you."

I asked her aunt, "What is this child?" And she answered, "We cannot go out with only one coat, because if she sees in the street a child who has no coat, she wants to take hers off. On one day which was cold, we forbade her to do that and she went to bed with a high fever." She was a baby and she was already generous. Her aunt died and I do not know what became of her.

Allegra Markevitch with Nadia Boulanger and her famous birthday cake. Photo courtesy Fontainebleau Alumni Association.

The carp pond at Fontainebleau Palace. Photo courtesy of Clarence Brodeur.

Although she was honored late in life in Europe as a member of the French Legion of Honor, a Commander of the British Empire and similar titles from Poland, Belgium, and Monaco, perhaps the greatest monument to her life was one she consciously sought from the city of Paris. On the fiftieth anniversary of her sister's death, the small intersection in front of 36 Rue Ballu was officially renamed as Place Lili Boulanger.

By her ninetieth birthday, her body had weakened. She was blind, but her mind was clear, and her teaching continued. Marion Touron-Branly, director of the School of Fine Arts at Fontainebleau, wished to pay Nadia a special tribute on the grounds of the Palace that she loved and adored. Requesting to be called *Nadijeda Ernestovna,* in a strict Russian manner, she was taken to the side of the carp pond adjacent to the Louis XV wing of the chateau. This party, on August 13, 1977, was a culmination of all the celebrations of her life. Speeches were prepared, soloists played, and an ensemble from the Menuhin School in England performed. In the exquisite gardens of the palace, the trees were covered with small lights, and gladiolas decorated all the tables, which held smoked salmon, caviar, pastries and champagne. The birthday cake was an enormous white basket.

When it became dusk, ninety white candles were put afloat independently on the pond. Then Napoleon's Pavillion in the center of the pond was flooded with light. Marion Touron-Branly made the introductory speech and Emil Naoumoff and Professor Stalanowski played a special composition for the event. Finally, three highly decorated classical balloons in blue and white were released over the pond into the clear summer air. Emil, her last young protégé, a Romanian, walked with Nadia slowly and silently from this touching encomium.

Our memories are subjective, our techniques and disciplines are objective. Mademoiselle disliked speaking of herself and saw no use in others doing so. Thus, let this book be not a simple tribute to her own greatness, but a tributary into the complex generations of the future. Let her memory be a statue that can remind, even those who did not know her, that rigor, discipline and enthusiasm are the paths to freedom.

Not all of Boulanger's students became devoted to her pedagogical style or musical tastes. Her intensity and acute concentration could easily push students beyond their psychological extremities. The rigid technical requirements occasionally brought more of a breakdown of attitude for her students rather than a breakthrough toward an independent creative freedom. Phillip Glass developed his own natural musical style after years of study with Mademoiselle. He left her to expand his musical manners through Indian music and Eastern methods of harmony, later continuing toward masterful minimalistic forms.

Donald Harris of the University of Hartford wrote in detail of his own inner pugnaciousness toward her immovable stance on compositional techniques in an article, *The Student Who Broke Away:*

> *What used to anger me most were her references to American culture. I remember two occasions when she would point her finger and say, "Harris! Europe is Athens, and America, Rome." How I hated the sounds of those words. Every fiber in my body rose up against this arbitrary dismissal of the very culture I loved the most. If we had not yet produced our Beethoven, Bach or Mozart, I was certain we would.*

Boulanger leaving the Jeu de Paume *in Fontainebleau, 1975.*

My argument that we had been around for less than 200 years, as op-
posed to the Parisian claim of 2,000 years of cultural history, was to
no avail whatsoever. Mademoiselle stuck to her opinion that America
was of lesser cultural importance than Europe, that most everything it
had created emulated Europe, and that, by extension, everything it
would create would have no innate personality since it would be
culturally dependent upon Europe. This had been the lot of Rome,
and America was simply following suit. History, as she suggested, was
repeating itself. The disagreement was too great. At the end of the
year I left to pursue my studies elsewhere. I wrote Mademoiselle a let-
ter, received a reply, and believed a chapter in my life to be closed.

Twenty-five years later, every fiber still fights for the same convictions
I held previously, but sometimes I wonder if Mlle. Boulanger's
predictions may not turn out to be correct. Obviously, I have no
desire to see it prevail, and I hope against hope that today is only a
momentary lapse in our history and not a continuing degradation.
This may be the only lesson I have learned from this great lady with
whom I had so little in common, but for whom, as the years have
gone by, I have learned to have deeper and greater respect. I would
prefer to have remembered her for something else.

Father Edward J. McKenna of Chicago studied with Mademoiselle, lived at 36 Rue Ballu, and became a trusted confidant. While visiting France during the last days of her life, he recalled their last meeting and the Requiem mass.

Our final meeting was brief in those rooms on Rue Ballu that had already been in mourning for half a century. I gave my name, reminded her of the masses we had offered so long ago in that very room, and told her of that great journey for which she was eminently prepared. When I finished certain prayers "for the dying" and blessed her, her face brightened and unseeing eyes turned in my direction. That marvellous sense of hearing, that perfect pitch was intact until the end. To enter into that moment of genuine Adieu is to pursue the mystical. As a priest who ministered to his mother as she breathed her last breath, I felt honored to do the same for the finest woman musician of the century, who was after all both teacher and confidante. I would like to say there was music or song in that farewell, but what she loved most in religious music was Gregorian, and the Requiem was still ten days away.

Thus it was the Gregorian Requiem that served as Introit, Sanctus and Agnus Dei at the solemn concelebrated Mass at 10:30 a.m. at the Trinité on October 26, 1979. At the Offertory a superb string ensemble played an arrangement of a Renaissance motet by Byrd. For Communion there were Lili's final works, ever appropriate. Prince Rainier and Princess Grace, lifelong friends of hers, recited the "Notre Père". The enormous floral displays from Yehudi Menuhin, Sir Clifford Curzon and Leonard Bernstein, the innumerable friends and admirers brightened the liturgy in that rather austere church. Not the least important remark in Père Carreé's eulogy pointed out the universality of that gathering and the presence of the American priests and former student. It was her geniality that he emphasized being rooted in her unshakable faith, her ability to reach out beyond the rigorous specialization of her life and touch so many different hearts. Geniality was her pastoral manner; music was her business. God, who is all love and beauty, was her focus.

I was left to me to perform the interment rites at Montmartre Cemetery, where the greatest artists of France rest. Of course, it rained. My words, my prayers, mostly spontaneous, were recited by her friends and former students. But the only song was the Requiem chant for rest . . . rest eternal.

NADIA ADIEU!

The Palace of Fontainebleau, 1972. Photo © Douglas Lyttle.

60

"THOSE MEN WHO HAVE LIT UP THE ROAD *for eternity were always alone in the midst of the multitude, alone among loved ones, alone in seeing too high, too far, alone in some terrifying solitude, because the questions that reared up between them and the unknown are scarcely conceivable to us.*"

NADIA BOULANGER

Nadia Boulanger 1935. Photo courtesy John Donald Robb.

Words

OF THE MASTER TEACHER

"WHAT IS DONE WITHOUT JOY IS ZERO."

"NOTHING is better than music. When it takes us out of time, it has done more for us than we have the right to hope for. It has broadened the limits of our sorrowful lives; it has lit up the sweetness of our hours of happiness by effacing the pettinesses that diminish us, bringing us back pure and new to what was, what will be and what music has created for us."

"In music everything is prolonged, everything is edified and when the enchantment has ceased, we are still bathed in its clarity. Solitude is accompanied by a new hope between pity for ourselves, which makes us more indulgent and more understanding, and the certitude of finding something again, that which lives forever in music."

"I AM always interested to see the development of life. You may follow it or not, you may agree or not, but you must know what is going on . . . ."

"EYES are to the body what intelligence is to the soul. Therefore it is necessary to have eyes, but that is not enough. You must look, but that is not enough; you must see."

"In music, the process can only be accomplished if you teach a student to love the preliminary disciplines that are necessary to composing. You can even make a student aware of the extraordinary need for concentration. I don't mean that he must work alot, but whenever he is working, he must really work."

"Let me quote my friend Paul Valéry: He who wants to write down his dreams owes it to himself to be awakened. That is the answer."

Nadia Boulanger 1969.

"THERE IS NOTHING boring in life except ourselves. The most humble work does not have to be boring. I remember the old woman who cleaned the floor in my place in Gargenville. She died a few years ago. Every day I think of her with the most profound respect and with greatest reverence. She was eighty years old. One day she knocked at my door and said, 'Mademoiselle, I know you don't like to be disturbed, but the floor, it shines in such a way. Come and see.'"

"Now I think of her always. In my mind, Stravinsky and Madame Duval will always appear before the Lord for the same reason. Each has done what he does with all his consciousness. When I said to Mme. Duval the same thing she did not know exactly what I meant. But when I said it to Stravinsky, who knew her, he said 'How you flatter me, for when I do something, I have something to gain. I *have* something. But she, she has only the work to be well done.' "

"As I said, it is essential to have a solid technique, but technique alone is nothing. You need something else, I can't define what that something else is, but I can feel it in a student. I know only one thing: You must always work . . . . work with integrity. If a genius is there, the rest will take care of itself."

"THE ONLY THING you can do is try to understand a person and then discuss with him what he has not done. Really, you cannot develop or change anything in anybody. You can respect what he is and try to make him a true picture of himself."

"As a teacher, my whole life is based on understanding others, not on making them understand me. What the student thinks, what he wants to do — that is the important thing. I must try to make him express himself and prepare him to do that for which he is best fitted."

André Marchal and Nadia Boulanger, 1969. Studio Théo.

Artur Rubenstein and Nadia Boulanger during a piano master class, 1958. Studio Théo.

"TIME IS TIME. No second comes again. Make a religion of this. Read and think in advance. Joy but not obligation in movement."

"I WORK today because I have today at my disposal."

"Remember the words of the poet: Tears are not made by sadness, but by the miracle of the right word in the right place."

"YOU MUST make your ears for each period of music."

"NOVELTY is what perishes quickest."

"SIGHT READING is like life. The important purpose is to come from the beginning and go to the end. Never stop. Never stop life. It must continue, even with a mistake, even if we think we repeat."

"DESIRE IS EVERYTHING. One can know everything, do everything, go everywhere, but without desire . . . It is nothing."

"I would rather a student had strong desires than none at all. There is something to work with. But afterwards, I must discover for each his own rhythm of effort. My terrible pace may not be his way. One can never dose them all with the same potion."

"WHAT IS IMPORTANT is not to define, but to act. One must try to do one's work with enough love and enough care to make it represent one's very best. The whole joy of being a human being is to realize the difficulty in reaching one's aim. The higher the aim, the greater the difficulty, and the greater our humility and joy. As for beauty — is it not mainly through beauty for service, of which there is no material reward or punishment, that we reach the spiritual art of our life which is the whole purpose of existence and its only goal?"

Nadia, 1925.
Courtesy of Louise Talma.

Nadia Boulanger 1928.
Photo courtesy Louise Talma.

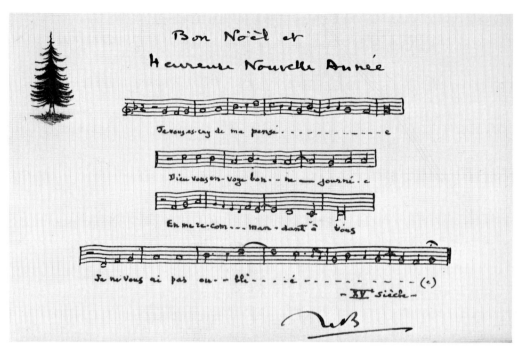

Handwritten Christmas card from Nadia Boulanger, 1938. Courtesy Harriet Ely.

"YOU MUST be a flaming passion if this music demands it. Ask, ask, ask. You cannot be satisfied by simply being here."

"YOU MUST satisfy curiosity, not awaken it. It makes a false vocation."

"WE MUST be happy to do music. We must live. We must be happy in sadness, for sadness has a reason. I must pay attention to life and not let it pass, without interest in life, even in its sadness."

"YOU SHOULD never listen to someone practice. That is their work and theirs alone."

"IT IS NOT SAD. It is a fact."

"A TEACHER must develop first consciousness, second memory and tools, and thirdly, expectation."

68

Stravinski and Boulanger at Fontainbleau, 1938. Courtesy of Nicholas Brill.

Conducting in the Jeu de Paume, *Fontainbleau, 1960. Studio Théo.*

"WHAT IS MEANT to be heard in music must be heard within you before anyone else can hear it. I cannot participate in music where the rhythm or line is forgotten."

"IT IS one thing to be gifted and quite another thing to be worthy of one's own gift."

"MAY I have the power to exchange my best with your best."

"YOU ARE ALL DEEP. It is the deepness of you I want to meet within me. This may bore you, but I do not care because some year you will remember, somehow."

70

"I AM your highest degree of tension. Listen to it in yourself."

"I DEMAND nothing of you. You must demand it of yourself."

"WHAT IS GREAT IS GREAT. We have no opinion on what is truly great."

"I AM FORTUNATE to have kept what I promised. I am sorry that words are not my kingdom and I am unable to explain anything. I want to tell you that life is a marvelous adventure, sometimes very hard. It must not have been easy for Mr. Johann Sebastian Bach in his life, but he had strength of life, vital power. The destructive incidents were only the outside expression of his life. The real expression brings us back, nearer to what is great and what is good. To awaken this joy in someone is a great joy. I thank the Lord that I can explain grammar to students. I can make him cheer if he has any kind of gift — and I can make him see — not to make him great, but to be a little more himself, a little better, a little more understanding and a little happier."

"YOU BELIEVE that I am a prophet. I feel that you ask me things that if I could answer, then the whole world would come to hear me talk. I do not know at all. I have my poor little ways of thinking about this subject, but very timidly, very shyly, it's too above me, you know."

"YOUR MIND does not listen, but your heart will remember."

"DO NOTHING FOR EFFECT. Do it for truth."

"ARRANGE YOUR LIFE to be able to answer fully to the given call. As soon as you will forget you are writing and first hear, then construct, balance check. You will find yourself in your element quite naturally. Of course, with struggles, days of misfortune, of defeat . . . but which are being an alive experiment."

"THOSE WHO ARE GREAT need to tell us so little. We must know how to listen and we will understand."

André Marchal and Boulanger at a master class in 1976. Photo Campbell.

"THERE IS NO CONTRADICTION between tradition and innovation, no barriers between craftmanship and passion."

"ONE MUST DO what is right, not just what is expected. It is good to admire, but not enough to appreciate."

"PEOPLE DO NOT SEE that the great men of today are all that will remain as a witness to themselves. To be among those who are not astonished or shocked or depressed by this second great war, and yet do something with it, who love it as their own time, is such a lesson. All work is in the present."

"GREAT MUSIC is not done for the crowd. No great art is. The crowd follows sometimes."

72

"PEOPLE CHANGE very little. There are always serious people and there are always frivolous people. In any case, we are much too close to today's activities to predict what will emerge. What would trouble me is if the young people lost their enthusiasm, their concentration, their power of choice and selection."

"Young people have great respect for technique. They must have. Music is technique, it is the only aspect of music we can control. Thus one's preparation for composing is not enough. A career without thorough training is inconceivable. Unfortunately, it sometimes happens. One can be free of the essential techniques of one's art only when it has been completely mastered."

"WHERE IT can't be played on the piano, do the best you can. Be sure to give the mood of the piece. Make the effort to give the spirit to the music. It is an effort. Keep the rhythm."

Mrs. Paul Valéry and Mademoiselle, 1964. Studio Théo.

Nadia Boulanger, 1975.

"ALL MUSIC MUST BE DRAMATIZED. Whether it be a masculine character or a feminine character . . . . *It must* have character or there is no life. Now forget what you have composed and be its character."

"False notes can be forgiven, false music cannot. Have confidence that you can do it. In life you are alive. Believe in life, it is your life. It is a question of vitality."

"FOR WHAT DO WORDS by themselves do? A written analysis of music may present a page of beautiful literature. It may be possible to put the listener into the mood to listen to music. But real music is sound, one sound after another, from where it has been to where it will go. There is no name for the music itself, the piece exists apart from every other. People know Debussy's *Faune* by its sound. It is an undeniable mystery . . . and a miracle, too."

74

"PLAY ALL your music in a way the audience will quite naturally feel intelligent."

"ART IS NOT EMOTION but a result from the manner in which emotion is expressed. The greatness of a work of art always depends on the judicious process employed by its creation. What is important is how it is made. The amateur must be able to understand this side of a composition as completely as its emotional aspects. The greater his comprehension and receptivity, the greater will be the music created at a given period. When the amateur is of the sort valuable to the creative artist, he uses his brain to temper his feelings. It is during the times during which emotion is under the control of the intellect that great art emerges."

"MUSIC SHOULD BE PLEASANT, gay, uplifting, enjoyable, if it is to fulfill its destiny. You think perhaps, that the Fauré *Sonata* and the Fauré *Requiem* are simple, that their substance is slight. That is not so, you do not know them. Like most rare and precious things, the exquisite quality of a work is not to be discerned all at once. It must be discovered."

"THE GREAT CONDUCTOR is always a despot by temperament and intractable in his ways. Few arts demand and develop the will more . . . . Few occupations put to the test one's patience, one's mastery of oneself and one's will more. The artist is obliged to keep his laughter and tears to himself. If they want to emerge, in spite of himself, then he must hide them or unleash them in someone else."

"ONE CAN ONLY BE FREE if the essential technique of one's art has been completely mastered."

"ALL THAT WE KNOW by heart enriches us and helps us find ourselves. The true personality is aided by the personality of others. That is why we must develop."

"Emotion without knowledge is perfectly acceptable. One cannot pretend to initiate the whole public in simply technical terms."

Nadia Boulanger, 1976.

"WE ARE OFTEN MISTAKEN about art. Art is not emotion. Art is the medium in which emotion is expressed."

"Without a strong cup to carry the emotion, it is only a curiosity. Great art can come to us only in strong cups. Without emotion, there is nothing to carry."

"I TRY TO GIVE THEM the means with which to work and make no effort to shape their writing. I endeavor to enlarge their vocabulary and to acquaint them with the etymology of the thing, but leave them to themselves when it comes to expressions. What a composer has to express is his own affair, not mine."

✓ Same w/writing

"I hold for strict technique along with personal freedom, probably at a 50/50 ratio. I view the composer in relation to his national culture: for first there must be humanity or nothing worthwhile can be spoken. And in turn the composer must discourse in phrasing and in the rhetoric particular to himself. For he must be more than a musician; he must be strong in the knowledge of his own country. If he is not full grown in that respect at first, he must mature later or otherwise he will never be heard."

"YOUR HANDS MUST be full of magnetism.
Put the fingers and mind to work, you will have music."

"This is Bartok, so think to the earth. You will see that Hungary is not so far away. You have put on the Hungarian costume, but you do not know how to wear it. It must come from the soul."

"EACH GESTURE must have integrity."

"YOU REALLY CANNOT DISCUSS TASTE, but you can discuss the facts. All above, do not permit yourself to laugh ironically, ever. Laugh with the student, let him laugh at himself pleasantly, but not in shame. That kills action. Action is the most important thing."

"LOOSE IS NOT BEAUTIFUL, loose is loose."

77

"BACH USES the circle of fifths over and over again, but oh, so nobly and with such eternal variety with passing notes. The circle of fifths is fundamental in Ravel's 'Tombeau de Couperin' as in the classics. It is the way you make your circle of fifths that counts. If you know your chords thoroughly in your mind and hands, then you can use them to modulate and vary them. A man who is very poetic, but knows no French cannot be a French poet. The same is true of a musician who wants to compose. He must learn the language of music, not only with his mind but also with his fingers."

"SOME PEOPLE have trouble through fright or shame. Nothing can be worse for the personality. It will stop the development of style and form. Many prefer to laugh at themselves in irony rather than discuss a tragedy."

"HAVE YOU THE COURAGE to have an opinion? One who has no opinion at all should be sent to sleep. If you do not learn to think, you will waste time and money buying the newspapers to see what others think."

"IT IS BETTER to confess that virtually nothing happens for which we are not ourselves more or less directly responsible. We should look for our part of the blame in each event."

"THE LAWS OF HARMONY and counterpoint are necessary to the development of the mind. All troubles come with students from the fact that they have not become familiar with the simple fundamentals. The fundamentals must be known without having to charge the memory."

"IT IS NOT ENOUGH to memorize the notes, you must sing every voice of the fugue. Sing the alto and omit it from your playing, then the tenor, then the bass, then the soprano, then the fugue is yours and you can easily permit it to be."

"THIS IS YOU, here in these few bars. It is really your music. But is this really what you want? With young composers detail is infinitely important and few pay enough attention to it. But let us go on. Words cannot speak of music and vice versa. It must be performed."

78

Aaron Copland and Nadia Boulanger, 1972. Photo © Douglas Lyttle.

"YOU MUST REMEMBER what St. Thomas Aquinas said to play this work.

> *To be aware of what is going on, one must feel the presence of the past, the presence of the present, and the presence of the future.*

To be this work, you must be its beginning, center and end all at once. Pay attention to all of it."

"THERE ARE THREE DISTINCT classes of musical amateurs. First there are those who possess only a love of music. They are fooled by their feelings. Secondly, there are amateurs born primarily to think, not feel. Their love of knowledge is likely to make them living encyclopedias. Finally, there is a minority blessed with the ability both to think and to feel. (These are the recipients of culture and it is of the greatest importance that they should receive it, since it is the quality of the amateur that permits works to be fully understood.) It is this third group that is indispensable to the creative musician. These are the ones who should be the recipients of culture because they are the ones ready to receive it. The quality of the amateur's reception of modern art is what permits a work to be fully understood."

"THERE ARE THREE CLASSIFICATIONS of applications from students: those without money and without talent; those I do not take; those with talent and without money: those I take; and those with talent and money: those I do not get."

"TRENDS ARE ALWAYS INTERESTING. But it always depends on who will handle these tools. Nothing depends on the system, everything depends on the musician. Stravinsky's use of the twelve-tone elements in *Canticum Sacrum* is not an experiment. It is an accomplishment."

"MUSIC WAS NOT INVENTED by the composer, but found."

"STRAVINSKY'S MUSIC satisfies one's mental faculties and yet at the same time touches the heart."

"THERE ARE DANGERS in atonal music. There is nothing to surprise one."

"EACH OF STRAVINSKY'S creations possesses a complete individual significance. His works as a whole reflect his whole personality. And yet he does not try to make his art express himself. And so it has been with composers in other important periods."

"AS LONG AS I am exacting, there is hope. If I am nice, that is a bad sign."

80

With a student at the American Conservatory, 1972. Photo © Douglas Lyttle.

With students in her Fontainebleau studio, 1966.

"PRACTICE THIS IMPOSSIBLE until it is accomplished. Then find your next impossible. Keep going and nothing will be difficult. Beat an even beat, count an odd beat, tap triplets to the even beat. You will see."

"FAURÉ WROTE this after the death of his father in 1886 and at the time of his mother's death in 1888. 'Now you must feel the grief, hope and faith in every line.' Here are tears of salvation, not death."

"YOU MUST KNOW the Nature . . . the nature. Mozart was not American, not Norwegian. He was Mozart. You must put on his nature. Stand on his earth. Now play."

"OURS IS NOT A period of 'best' but a period of trial — struggle. To be deep. You can be well dressed but still deep. Take the Mozart G Minor Symphony. It is light but is one of the great dramas of music."

82

"I ADMIRE THE MIRACLE of the human body and the young body with its almost infinite abilities and dominated by a young heart."

"DURING THE RELIGIOUS WARS when they were gouging out eyes, Orlando di Lasso was writing beautiful spiritual music. So today if we lose art, we may not have much left. Life is so acid, times are so tense, when it is a case of yes or no."

"I AM SO LUCKY to be so old now. I am so lucky that I am always with young people. It is the right combination."

"ONCE I WAS APPROACHED with an extraordinary request from a young Canadian girl. We were both very young, she was 19 and I about 17. She wanted piano lessons. I said very well, but what for? She said she would like to play the A-flat Ballade of Chopin. I agreed and asked her to play it. She said she did not know how to play the piano. I was amazed. She said she would practice until she knew it. Her mother was dead and she had played it very well. She knew she could never play it well, but wanted to play it the best she could for her father. I told her it was impossible. I was amused. So I played it for her, note by note, finger by finger, phrase by phrase. I told her every finger to move. It was long way, but she finally played it. It was a representation of great love, great confidence."

"I LOVE MY STUDENTS. I love to teach. Even now when I am not well, I have a crazy pleasure, always immense, for teaching."

"ONE MUST TRAIN THE MEMORY. To help train the memory you must have memory of eye, ear, hands and writing. One way to train it is to open a book and shut it after examining it for a few seconds, then see how much was seen. See if it can be played. Some people remember with their hands, but not with their head. There are many different kinds of memory."

"In order to train your memory, you must learn the different clefs, the relation of notes by actual movements. Correct observation is the first step. If you see vividly, you will remember more clearly, so be precise."

"REMEMBER THE POET VALÉRY:

*Words are adapted to great rhythms. . . . Great rhythms
absorb words.*"

"Things in music are not difficult, just unexpected."

"NOW YOU MUST LEARN the basics. It is so simple. you must see it is simple. Memorize the two volumes of the Bach Preludes and Fugues. That sounds difficult. It is not. Please, only one measure a day, one bar only. Now it is contagious and simple. In two years, you shall know it. It is simple, so do not look for the difficult."

"You must give each note life, your life. You must sacrifice, you must learn to give yourself to music. Then you will make it live. Then you will be able to make other people understand music."

"YOU MUST KNOW how to make in yourself a complete silence. Each of you in my mind is fated. You were born, you will live, you will die. Even to try is an achievement. Giving yourself completely is such a faith."

"IN THE SILENCE, I have either everything or nothing. I am old, I am tired for seventy five years. When you are not awake, I am weary, but when you are awakened, it is a privilege. It is so beautiful, this human mind."

"TO PERFORM ITS DUTY, which is to govern, the mind must have been trained in such a way that nothing can escape its control. This implies ears able to catch sound, isolated as well as superimposed or in linear succession, to feel rhythm and eventually to make the complex structure of the work as a whole perceptible."

"In order to obey the commands of the mind, the fingers, the hands, the arms must have achieved such a degree of independence and skill, such variety of touch, of such delicacy, a speed and strength, that they can all at once perform everything which is required."

84

In the Jeu de Paume, *awaiting a concert, 1972.*

"The mind and body should have been granted natural faculties. That goes without saying. But with the gifts alone, one cannot go very far. It is important to remember that the greater the gifts, the greater must be the character, the power of the work, the conscience, the moral and spiritual value of him to whom they were given. I know 'Unto every one that hath shall be given and he shall have abundance' (Matthew 25), but this is not achieved without great labor and patience. It cannot come without great love and great respect from the one who received."

Serving on a master jury in Fontainebleau, 1959.

"MANY DO NOT HEAR. I must persuade them and that is difficult. They must know that freedom rests upon what they hear spontaneously and what they can write down."

"THE GROWTH OF TALENT is unpredictable, certainly, but the ear . . . if there is no ear . . . (if I sing 'Do' and the student sings 'Fa') then I am obliged to say: It will displease you or make you sad for a while, but it is better I tell you now . . . you are no musician."

"LEARN THESE THINGS so thoroughly that you don't have to remember them."

86

"EDUCATION AND CULTURE in our day are becoming superficial. The old people used to memorize Greek and Latin and English verse. Gifts and imagination are important, but you can't train these. However, they are no good without roots in knowledge. Things are becoming hard nowadays that were once considered easy, such as improvisation, reading from a figured bass, transposition and reading at sight. If you have imagination to do things but you can't do them, you are a slave. You make a child eat what is served. You must make the students learn what they must. But make it as pleasant as you can. If people were made happy by being allowed to do as they wish, they really are not happy. Effort and mastery make for happiness. Discipline leads to technique. Common language makes for common understanding, but not if each person tries to invent his own language. The question is: where am I the most free? The answer is where I have worked hardest, where I have tyrannized."

"GREAT ART LIKES CHAINS. The greatest artists have created art without bonds. Or else they have created their own chains."

"THE EAR IS EVERYTHING: We must give children tones, pitch recognition, as we give them language or the symbols of mathematics. And we must begin early. I trained the little boy of my houseman when he was only three. Each day, for only a minute at first, when I would play 'Do' he would sing 'Do' and I would sing 'Mi' and he, 'Mi', then 'Re' and so forth. If he would make a mistake, I would act astonished and ask: "What is the matter? Are you sick today?" By this method, all children can be given an accurate ear, whether or not they become musicians. Not everyone who writes a good letter is a writer."

"IN ROMANIA, they build houses to hold the largest number of people in the smallest possible space. Here in this palace, I have room to breathe."

"TO LIVE YOU HAVE TO COUNT. One who counts best lives best. One should be a saint to be a true teacher. The eyes give food to the hands."

"HOW CAN YOU BE so weak with your music? Have you no backbone? Have you no pride? You must save your tears for important things. You know about my sister's death and how my mother died. Now, save your tears or you will have none left for the real tragedies."

"YOU MUST READ AT SIGHT every day. It must be a natural hunger. It is so terrible to force oneself to eat."

"MY MAIN CONCERN now is to develop the conscience of the musician, which is his ear."

"BE INGENIOUS. Find a way to make the student understand, but don't try after one year if he's not musical to make him what he is not."

"YOU MUST remember always what Rodin said:

We prepare forms for beauty, but we do not know whether it will come to live there."

"TO BE A COMPOSER and not a musician is a tragedy, it is to have genius and not talent."

"DON'T LOOK AT THE PIANO, do it in your mind first. Do it fifty times a day. It may take a month, a year, a lifetime to master what you want to do. Start slowly, then do it faster. Then do it by various interval jumps. A musician hears everything or he hears nothing. People who hear, do something with their lives and do it everyday. Schubert lived only thirty one years, but he wrote millions of notes."

"EVERYBODY WANTS TO HEAR WHAT I have to say about new music. I think there is too much talk. The trouble is that it is all talk about means, not enough about results. New means, new devices always come along: life goes on and one can never remain motionless. But without the spirit to put these means to some purpose, they become nothing but academic formulas."

"IT IS NOTHING to succeed if one has not taken great trouble, and it is nothing to fail if one has done the best one could."

"EACH PERIOD is different. But there is no progress in beauty. Beauty is beauty, where or when it occurs."

With Idil Biret, Turkish pianist. Courtesy of the Gilmore collection.

"IT GOES VERY SLOWLY. If only you can get a student to look around and
see. Once they begin to look around they will begin to develop. You
know what T.S. Elliot said of education, that the goal is to make us like
what we once disliked. The teacher must give a student 'sight' and teach
him how to listen. If they learn to listen, they will go on learning. Those
who continue to see and listen know happiness. When they stop, happiness falls short."

Nadia in Venice for the Stravinsky performance of The Rake's Progress, *1951. Photo courtesy of Ann Gilmore.*

"Do things, do, act. Make a list of the music you love, then learn it by heart. And when you are writing music of your own, write as you hear it inside and never strain to avoid the obvious. The person who does that is living outside of life. At your age it is bearable and when you are thirty it should be bearable. But at forty, it is unbearable."

"New students ask the same questions of me and I ask them the same questions.

The biggest question I was ever asked was by a small boy in Boston:

What constitutes a masterpiece?

It is so fortunate that no answer exists. To me genius is the greatest mystery of our existence. I can give you a few hints, but no firm answer."

"Everybody is obliged to earn his own bread, but it has offended me since I started teaching in 1904 and it shames me today. The way to eat and the way to teach are two absolutely separate questions. It is the spirit that counts, not the money."

"When you start to compose anything that is not already a part of your subconscious, part of your completely mastered knowledge, it's not going to be of any use to you."

"Keep at it. You are truly a composer. Avoid too great symmetry in your composing. If you were not married, I would say give it all up to composition."

"The only thing I can do is try to understand a person and then discuss with him what he has not yet done. Really, I can't develop or change anything, in anybody. I can respect what he is and try to make him a true picture of himself. It is between the teacher and the student to find out who you are."

"Fauré is to me a classic composer, and I find this classic spirit predominant in the Requiem. Others feel it differently, I know. To me it is very simple, very austere. Do you know how I discovered the spirit of this music? It was during a trip to Greece. I was there for only a few hours, but when I saw those great classic structures I understood Fauré for the first time. I find this spirit in Chopin, too, but very few people pay it any heed."

"The important thing is to do. If you can do something, it stands. It is not enough to know about something. You must try to do it, even if only poorly at first. Without craft and discipline, a student labors with wings clipped. Sometimes when I bid a student goodbye, I say

We have tried to give you a technique. Now let's see you go out and use it for what you have come to say.

Without discipline, there can be no freedom."

"What if I say that this composer, this paper is dead. What are we doing here? Anyone can get into this frame of mind, negation of life and energy. If one can't react, one is ill. Even if ill, you must be sure of yourself. If the teacher gets mad enough, the child will do it."

"The child fell and got up eighty-five times. You could almost see the child saying, *I can do it.* You could feel the excitement. That's the difference between life and death. Take Stravinsky. Before the Lord he is a miserable invalid, but he is alive. Never accept defeat. Being alive, one is never defeated. Attitude means the difference between mediocrity and something one thousand times better. Before a masterpiece, a part of the divine, one should be in a passion. Don't be like him who slept when the Lord came. How can I wake you?"

"There is no substitute for discipline in music. You must go back to the basic concept of discipline in this art, and the more engrossed you become in the history of music and strict academic form, the more free you will be as you compose later on."

92

One of Nadia Boulanger's last classes in her Fontainebleau apartment.

Clifford Curzon, Nadia Boulanger, Jean Casadesus, 1959. Studio Théo.

Nadia Boulanger, 1972. Photo © Douglas Lyttle.

"I TRY TO ARRANGE MY WORK AND do it well. That is all. I try to keep myself out of these big questions. As a teacher, my whole life is based on understanding others, not on making them understand me. What the student thinks, what he wants to do, *that* is the important thing. I must try to make him express himself and prepare him to do that for which he is best fitted."

94

"HOW DO YOU DO? I have just finished a class and I am tired beyond words. I cannot speak with you after all. I never pay attention to my health, but now I have been stopped. Anyway, I have nothing to say about myself. I am interested in the student. The place of the teacher depends on the student. But everything depends on you. What do you ask?"

"MUSIC CAN BE VERY SAD. Yet we must always be happy to do music. We must live. We must be happy in sadness, for sadness has a reason. Pay attention to life and do not let it pass without interest in it, even in its sadness."

"BAD MUSIC IN CHURCH is a bad thing. Some of the greatest of all music is church music. The music of the Catholic Church makes one forget self. It is ridiculous to use the pronoun "I" in Chartres Cathedral. There is a revival of church music today. The great ages of mankind have their roots in the spiritual life. It is interesting that many young men today are doing religious music."

"ELECTRONIC MUSIC is an experiment and one must encourage research. Is it anti-artistic? They say that about the new music of all epochs. I have a letter Gounod wrote to my father asking if he, like so many people, thought the dissonances in *Faust* were intolerable."

"I don't know what the modern trend is. All times have been modern. Valéry said:

Novelty is that which is most perishable.

Cocteau said:

Fashion is what is outmoded.

On art there are no generations, only individuals. There are today very important works and very poor ones as in all epochs. Those who deplore our epoch ignore history."

"ONE CANNOT DISCUSS WITHOUT having stated. To make a melody have an effect, it must be clearly stated."

"A CRESCENDO is an inner thing. It must be easy to the ear. It is like coming up the beautiful staircase outside the apartment in the Palace at Fontainebleau. The stones are beautiful, they are smooth, their rhythm is so intelligent. The curves are for the ease of the feet. A crescendo is for the ease of the ears."

"WITHOUT ORDER there can be no inner satisfaction. Without inner satisfaction, there can be no freedom. Without freedom there can be no joy."

"GREATNESS IS not a question of quality, but of proportion."

"THE GREATEST JOY in being a human being is to realize the difficulty in reaching one's aim. The higher the aim, the greater the difficulty and the greater our joy and our humility."

"MORE OFTEN than not, we talk of things that we scarcely know, we often discuss things of which we have no knowledge, and in reality we are often ignorant of things which we think we love."

"RETIREMENT? I do not know what that is. One works or one cannot work . . . that would be death."

"I FEEL LIKE A CHILD who is watching a clock. When the hand moved the child said,

I am older but I do not feel any older.

I never think of age. I have not time. I work."

96

Nadia Boulanger with Annette Dieudonné, her closest associate and persona grata. *Photo © Douglas Lyttle.*

In council with American students, 1972. Photo © Douglas Lyttle.

Writings
OF THE MASTER TEACHER

Lectures on Modern Music[1]

Modern French Music

LET US AGREE that by our title we mean French music of the post-Franckian period, the period inaugurated by the works of Fauré and Debussy. The classification is, of course, arbitrary, for naturally there is no sharp line of demarcation between the music of today and the music of yesterday. Music, like life, is in constant evolution. Its transformation goes on incessantly, but the process is so gradual that, for the most part, we remain quite unconscious of the nature and extent of the changes which are taking place before our very eyes. We are too inattentive, our minds too passive, to observe or record, to say nothing of understanding, them. It is so much easier to rest contented with what we have already acquired than to change ever so slightly those routine but profound habits of thought and feeling which govern our life, and by which we live so blissfully because so unconsciously. This mental inertia is, perhaps, our greatest enemy. Insidiously it leads us to assume that we can renew our lives without renewing our habits; that we can listen to the music of Stravinsky with ears attuned only to the harmonies of Beethoven and Wagner. But we cannot.

Consequently no one can "explain" modern music, make it, by some miracle, immediately intelligible to people who have never heard a note of it or who will not make the effort to accustom themselves, by prolonged application, to new sonorities and, therefore, to new habits of hearing. All one can do is to try to stimulate the curiosity of those who have yet to make their first acquaintance with a modern score and to render more intelligent and precise the appreciation of those who have already learned to love a world of beauty in which they are not yet quite at home.

The harmony of modern music, especially its dissonance, is, of course, the chief stumbling block. That is natural and unavoidable, and the difficulties which it presents should not be underestimated nor, on the other hand, exaggerated. The obstacle is obviously of a technical nature; it is a question of language, a matter of vocabulary and syntax and is therefore to be mastered like any linguistic problem — by the processes of mental and aural assimilation. To learn to speak a new language is difficult; but

[1] Three lectures delivered under the auspices of the Lectureship in music at the Rice Institute, in February, 1925, by Mlle. Nadia Boulanger, of Paris, France. The author gratefully acknowledges the kindness of Mr. Howard Hinners in editing the stenographic report of the lectures for publication.

it is relatively easy to learn to understand it. So it is with modern harmony. At a first hearing, Stravinsky's "Sacred Rites of Spring" seems a mere uncoördinated mass of sound. But listen to it again and again and gradually the sense of confusion disappears. Little by little the "catching" quality of its themes and the electric force of the rhythms emerge, and the music becomes a thing so full of life and power that you marvel at your previous bewilderment.

"The dissonances of to-day are the consonances of tomorrow" — an immemorial commonplace of musical history which every one knows in theory but whose force becomes apparent only by personal experience. To us it seems incredible that the interval of a third was once considered harsh or that Monteverdi (1568-1643) should have had difficulty in securing *droit de cité* for the chord of the dominant seventh.

Yet we all know that such was the case and that such will always be the fate of every new "dissonance".

The history of harmony is the history of the development of the human ear, which has gradually assimilated, in their natural order, the successive intervals of the harmonic series:

The platitudinous validity of the statement becomes obvious by comparison of the harmonic series with the following table, which gives — with only approximate accuracy — the chief diatonic chords in use during the successive periods of musical history.

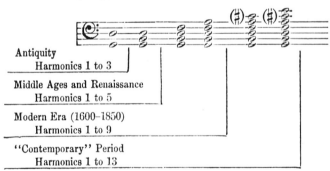

Antiquity Harmonics 1 to 3	
Middle Ages and Renaissance Harmonics 1 to 5	
Modern Era (1600–1850) Harmonics 1 to 9	
"Contemporary" Period Harmonics 1 to 13	

At first, some of these chords, notably the last four, were employed only on certain degrees of the scale, but now they are all in current use on every degree. Furthermore, composers no longer hesitate to alter (viz, to sharp or flat) any note, or any combination of notes, in any chord, a practice which is likewise justifiable by the phenomenon of resonance the moment one admits the chord of three notes, whose combined harmonic series give (enharmonically, viz., with F# =

100

G♭, etc.) every note of the chromatic scale.

But such *a posteriori* apologies are rather ridiculous and must not be used to prove more than they actually do; namely, that there are no acoustical reasons why any combination of notes should not be used harmonically, that is, as a chord. Whether or not a given chord is beautiful, is another question, of an aesthetic, not a physical, order. The beauty of a chord, or of any other musical element, depends on its context. As Voltaire says, "The real art is in the *à propos*". *(Le grand art est dans l'à propos.)* Certain formulae of chord progression are quite boresome when they occur in the music of a third-rate composer, but coming from the pen of a Fauré, the same locutions take on, by some miracle, the highest and most moving qualities of beauty. Why that should be we do not know, and do not need to know. It is one of the many mysteries of art which elude all efforts at analysis.

In the preceding table, all the chords are formed by the superposition of thirds, but in modern music we are obliged to recognize other methods of chord construction. Scriabine, for instance, uses (excessively, perhaps) a chord based on the superposition of fourths:

Debussy frequently adds a sixth and a ninth to major triads, one of the many

examples in modern music of so-called "unresolved appoggiaturas", that is, of notes foreign to a chord, which do not resolve, as in the classics, or to integral notes of the chord. To consider such notes as non-harmonic tones is probably inaccurate, for they have gradually become part and parcel of the chord to which they were grafted. In short, they form new chords whose principles of formation have yet to be deduced and formulated.

More important, however, than the invention of new chords, is the use of other than our usual major, minor, and chromatic scales. Most people know that the

whole tone scale, is of frequent occurrence, for example, in the music of Debussy, but perhaps they are less conscious of the influence on modern harmony of the old church modes (themselves a survival of the antique Greek modes), especially the following:

These modes have, of course, been preserved in the Gregorian Chant, which is still the official music of the Catholic Church, and also in many of the countless European folk songs collected with such enthusiasm during the last forty years. A few examples will suffice to show the reality, if not the extent, of the influence:

FIRST MODE

THIRD MODE[2]

FIFTH MODE

---

[1] I am indebted to Messrs. Rouart Lerolle, Sénart Hamelle, Fromont, Durand, Heugel, Mathot, Chester, Musique Russe, Bussel and Henn for the liberty of reproducing the examples cites in these Essays.

[2] In modern uses of this mode, the dominant is usually changed from the sixth to the fifth degree of the scale.

102

SEVENTH MODE

Debussy, *Mandoline*

NINTH MODE

Ravel, *Trio*[1]

Equally characteristic are passages like the following, where, though it is not dominated by an single mode and though it contains modern characteristics, the harmony is nevertheless modal in its origins:

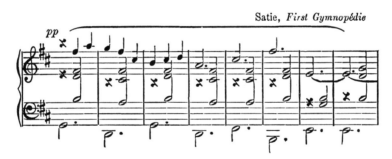

Satie, *First Gymnopédie*

Fauré, *At the Cemetery*

dolce e sereno

Heu-reux qui meurt i - ci, Ain- si que les oi-seaux des champs!

---

[1] The second theme of the first movement. The first theme is in the key of *A* minor with the sixth degree raised. In other words, both themes are based on scales having a common tonic, *A*, contrast being attained not, as in the classics, by a change of *key*, but by a change of *mode*.

Various oriental and defective (five-note) scales are likewise to be found in modern music and we shall have occasion to refer to them specifically in our discussion of the works of Roussel and Debussy.[1]

Recent composers, notably, Debussy, Schmitt, Roussel and Ravel, have devoted considerable attention to rhythmical problems, and their compositions contain many significant innovations in this domain. But to avoid repetition, it will be better to leave detailed discussion of this aspect of modern music for our lecture on Stravinsky.

I am sorry to have remained so long on purely technical ground. My only justification for so doing is that the main difficulty which modern music presents, not only to the layman but to the trained musician as well, is the difficulty inherent in the technical structure of its language. When once the language has been mastered, the "problem" of modern music becomes non-existent. It is impossible therefore to have too much technical knowledge. On the contrary, one never has enough.

Before passing on to our study of individual composers, may I say that it is only with regret and because they are naturally excluded by the limits of my subject, that I refrain from giving prolonged attention to the works of various Italian, Russian, German and other European composers. France has always been quick to recognize beauty and merit wherever they happened to be found[2] and I feel almost as though I were being unfaithful to the traditions of my country in not speaking of such men as de Falla, Malipiero, Szymanowski, Bartok, Schoenberg, etc. Their work is of first-rate significance and I am sorry that we can give it only passing mention instead of the detailed study which it deserves.

Fauré, Debussy and Stravinsky[3] are, of course, the chief figures in the musical history of the last thirty-five years. The work of Debussy and Stravinsky is known, if it is not always understood, the world over; but Fauré, who is perhaps the greatest of the three, is still practically unknown outside of France.

The simple facts of his life are quickly told. He was born in Pamiers (Ariège) on May 13, 1845, and educated in Paris at the École Niedermeyer. This last detail is of some importance because of the emphasis which that institution laid on training in the church modes and Gregorian Chant and because of the rather special manner in which it taught harmony, a manner which favored the use of altered chords and consequently encouraged those subtle allusions to remote keys that are so characteristic of Fauré's music. "Another main feature in the organization of the school", as Fauré himself said, "was that . . . instruction in the humanities was given hand in hand with the musical training and, . . . being run on the dormitory system of a boarding school, there was less scattering and dispersion of

---

[1] For a detailed account of the characteristics and evolution of modern harmony, see Charles Koechlin's masterly essays in Lavignac's *Encyclopédie de la Musique et Dictionnaire du Conservatoire*, 2° partie Vol. I; also Casella's admirable book on *The Evolution of Music*.

[2] In fact, she has sometimes been even too generous in this respect and has frequently recognized foreign merit before, and at the expense, of native achievements.

[3] These last two composers have been left for separate study in the succeeding lectures.

one's time and forces, less of that counsel coming from left and right, which is generally as fatal as it is contradictory, and finally, simply from the standpoint of music, there were fewer pernicious contacts".

His course of study completed, Fauré began his career as an organist, first in Rennes, later in Paris, at various churches, and finally at the Église de la Madeleine. In 1896 he was appointed professor of composition at the Paris Conservatoire, and nine years later became its director, a position which he held until 1920. Distinction followed distinction: he was elected to the Institute (1909) and given the grade of Commander of the Legion of Honor (1910)[1]. Several years later, the entire nation in the persons of the President of the Republic, the Premier and members of the cabinet, did him national homage during a special celebration held in his honor at the Sorbonne, a distinction that has been conferred on only one other person — Pasteur. Fauré died November 3, 1924, and was buried with all the pomp and splendor suggested by the phrase "funérailles nationales".

The man himself was extraordinary in his utter normality and simplicity, his unaffected goodness and kindliness of spirit. As Vuillermoz has said, "No artist has ever been more intensely, more profoundly loved. Great geniuses of the past have been given more solemn tributes of admiration, have called forth more demonstrative enthusiasm; they have acted with more intensity on the crowd and known a more universal and noisy fame; but none of them, in departing, have

made hearts grieve more painfully". It was impossible to know Fauré without loving him. The greater his renown, the more unconscious did he become of his own glory. As some one has said, "The man was so perfectly simple, that he seemed not to understand what people meant when they spoke of his simplicity". During his long years of professorship at the Conservatoire, never, in any class, did he let fall one word about himself or his work. The testimony of his pupils in this respect is unanimous. Had they not become acquainted with his music through the natural channels of the concert hall and the publishing house, they would never have known that Fauré, the teacher, was Fauré, the composer.

The atmosphere of his classroom, as I can testify from personal experience, was one of sanity and freedom, quite exempt from dogmatism and that narrow spirit of sect and school which we associate with even the best of educational institutions. As a teacher, he seemed to have but one principle: to understand his pupils, to adapt himself to their individual personalities and help them to find their own particular road to artistic self-realization. Distinguished musicians of opposing temperament and talents — Ravel, Schmitt, Roger-Ducasse, Aubert, Enesco, Koechlin, etc. — lived in the shadow of his personality without ever feeling the slightest sense of constraint. It was he who understood them and not they who had to understand him.

Like Mozart, Fauré is essentially a "musician's composer". The unique concentration of his style, his refinement and his grace are of the sort that sum up centuries of previous culture and development, which can be loved by any sensitive spirit,

[1] He was later promoted to the highest rank which the Legion of Honor offers.

but which only the trained musician can perhaps fully appreciate. For a foreigner the problem is perhaps even more difficult, for Fauré's music, like the dramas of Racine, is essentially French. Before its deceptive elegance, an Anglo-Saxon or a German sometimes feels those movements of impatience and irritation which the music of Brahms or Mahler tends to provoke in a Frenchman.

But in all such cases of national differences, longer acquaintance is an easy and a certain remedy, and in the end one finds oneself loving the very qualities which at first seemed so repellent. Also we must remember that, as Gide has said, "it is in being the most individual that one is the most universal".

The simplicity of Fauré's music has deceived even his compatriots. For many of them, Fauré is still a mere "charming musician" and nothing more, for, to be sure, his music, like the music of Mozart again, is the very quintessence of charm. But its charm is the charm of the aristocrat; it is the cloak of discretion and restraint that go with gentle manners and high breeding. For Fauré, in spite of his humble origins — his father was an inspector of primary schools in the provinces — is a patrician. His smiling suavity disdains all violence of mood or gesture and shuns the solemn effects of oratory and eloquence. He is never agressive, but conceals his strength beneath the quiet force of the unemphatic voice and the untroubled serenity of a soul that has found inner peace and certitude.

The technical characteristics of his music? They are difficult to discover and, because of their utter naturalness, embarrassing to state. The tonality, chords, rhythms and forms which Fauré uses are the same as they were when he first began to serve music, but, in his hands, these ordinary elements have become precious. Insensibly, year by year and work by work, he made them so perfectly his own that, old when he was young, they were still young when he was old. Even now, when he is dead and gone, they have lost no whit of their freshness, of their perennial charm.

Fauré has been called "the most suave of revolutionaries", and the epithet is just and merited. The syntax of modern harmony owes more to his music than we as yet realize. His vocabulary, to be sure, is the vocabulary of every one, the vocabulary of the classics: triads, seventh chords and an occasional ninth; but in his work these routine harmonies follow each other in a manner so distinctive, so ineffably personal, that they seem quite new, entirely original. The extraordinary ease and freedom which characterize, as in the following measures, his use of seventh chords,

Soir [1]

Vois! le der-nier rayon a-go-nise à tes ba - gues.

106

prepared the way for countless later liberties in Ravel and Debussy and clearly foreshadow the latter composer's manner of connecting chords of the ninth.

But, needless to say, in spite of some such minor technical resemblances, the harmony of Fauré and the harmony of Debussy are radically different. Harmony, for Fauré, is an element of design, whereas Debussy tends to conceive it rather as a source of color. Fauré etches in even the most subtle of his modulations with the sharp, fine lines of a pen. You never know to what key he is leading you, but when you reach your tonal destination, there is never any doubt as to its location. Indeed, you feel almost as though it would have been impossible to have gone elsewhere and you wonder only at the beauty of the voyage and at the skill of your guide who, in coming, has led you so quickly and surely through so many lands. The subtlety of Fauré's transitory modulations, the ease and naturalness with which he alludes to the most remote keys, are the mind's sheerest delight. Take, for example, a passage like the following: One knows not what to admire most in such harmony: the richness and accuracy of its allusions to foreign keys or the deftness with which it returns to the point from which it started.

La Parfum Impérissable

As the above citations show, Fauré, like Wagner, is one of the few composers who conceive tonality as a mobile and not a static state. Yet there is no direct filiation between the two men. One of the most extraordinary aspects of Fauré's music and one that says much for the power and independence which lurk beneath the charm of his personality, is that never can one say that such or such a piece was written under the influence of

[1] This particular song, it is true, is a late work and dates from 1900, but the same characteristics of harmonic progression are to be found in germ (but for that reason, none the less unmistakably) in the early compositions.

such and such a composer. Yet Fauré witnessed the rise and decline of reputations like Wagner, Franck, Strauss, Debussy, and lived to see the beginning of Stravinsky's fame. He took an active and sympathetic interest in their music but never was in the slightest danger of losing his artistic equilibrium, his natural independence of style. Strange as it may seem, he owes most to Gounod and Bach,[1] to the delicacy and suavity of the one and to the other's incomparable sense of self-unfolding melody.

Consider, for instance, the *Allegro Moderato* of the "Second Quintet". In reality, the entire movement represents a single, long line. Cadences there are, many plagal, two or three perfect, most of them deceptive; but very few of them, until the last pages of the coda, have the punctuative value of a period. Most of them are commas or at best, semicolons. Consequently, first, transition and secondary themes, development, recapitulation, and coda constitute not so many sections of a sonata form, but a single, uninterrupted melody which grows and unfolds with miraculous fecundity and naturalness. The resulting impression of freshness and youth is incredible, coming, as it does, from the pen of an old man of seventy-six.

Ordinarily, it is sad to grow old, but not so with Fauré. To age, for him, meant a quiet process of selection, the gradual liberation of his spirit, which, by a long and joyfully accepted discipline, had eliminated all that was useless and ephemeral and freed itself of "every

earthborn care". One feels that he regarded death in much the same way as Bach regarded it, as a natural goal and not a danger, as a state to be desired rather than feared. Here the great Protestant cantor and Fauré, the Catholic, have "ascended to meet". Works, for instance, like Bach's Choral Prelude for Organ, "O Man, Bewail thy Grievous Sin", and Fauré's "Requiem",[2] are both inspired by a similar, mystical view of religion and death, a view so high and serene that, in its presence, differences of creed and dogma fade into insignificance.

The Church can absolve and sustain, but also judge and condemn us. Unlike Bach, Fauré has never given expression to this latter and menacing aspect of his faith. Religion, he understands more in the manner of the Gospel according to St. John, in the manner of Saint Francis and Fra Angelico, than of Bossuet or Saint Bernard. He finds in it a source of love, not of fear. If, as in the "Requiem", he sings of the grief which death inspires, it is a grief so near to God as to be wholly free from vain revolt or lamentation. What dominates the quite impersonal tenderness of the music, is the sense of certain pardon, the serene expectation of eternal rest.

This note of certainty, of inner peace, is never absent from his work and explains, in part, at least, the man's deep and abiding joy in life. Every note he wrote — even of the works which chant the soul's nostalgia for the other world — attests his love of life, his love of loving it and the keen delight he felt at the mere perception that an object was lovely or a line beautiful. In this and other respects,

[1] Saint-Saëns, his teacher and life-long friend, must also have initiated him into some of the secrets of logical and lucid form.

[2] Cf. also "O mort, poussière d'étoiles".

he is Greek rather than Christian. He has the Greek's sense of measure and sobriety. Like Plato, he feels a sort of ecstasy before the austere though sensuous beauty of form or line. Take "Danseuse" *(The Dancer)* the last song in "Mirages"; its cool, detached beauty suggests the chaste contours, the sharp and clear designs of a Greek vase. One is reminded of Valéry's phrase, "I look upon this woman who is walking and yet who gives me a sense of immobility". *(Je contemple cette femme qui marche et qui me donne le sentiment de l'immobilité.)*

Fauré is indeed an "Attic musician", and one might very well think that these lines from "Eupalinos",[1] which describe with such penetrating subtlety the spirit of Greek architecture, were intended rather for the composer of "Pénélope" — so vividly do they suggest his idea of modulation, his sense of balance and proportion: "Like those orators and poets of whom you were thinking a moment ago, he [the architect] knew, O Socrates, the virtue of imperceptible modulations. Before his delicately lightened masses, in appearance, so simple, no one was conscious of the fact that, by these insensible curves, these minute but all powerful inflexions and by these profound combinations of the regular and irregular which had been introduced, hidden and rendered as imperious as they were indefinable, he was being led to a sort of happiness. They made the moving spectator docile to their invisible presence, caused him to pass from vision to vision, from absolute silence to murmurs of pleasure in proportion as he advanced, retreated, or approached again to wander, moved

[1] Likewise by Valéry.

by its beauty, and the puppet of admiration, within the radius of the building. It is necessary, said this man of Megara, that my temple move men as they are moved by the objects of their love".

We have scarcely touched on the music itself. I would have preferred to play it rather than write about it, or, since that is impossible, to quote whole pages of Fauré's works. But lack of space forbids and I must content myself with enumerating — in an order which may facilitate making his acquaintance — the most characteristic of his compositions: "Les Berceaux" *(The Cradles),*[2] "Aurore" *(Dawn),*[3] "Les Roses d'Ispahan" *(The Roses of Ispanan),*[3] "Claire de Lune" *(Moonlight),*[3] "Au Cimetière" *(At the Cemetery),*[4] "Prison", "Soir" *(Evening),*[4] "La Bonne Chanson"[5] "Pelléas et Mélisande" (orchestral suite)[5] "Elégie" (Cello and piano),[5] Sixth,[5] Seventh[5] and Ninth[5] "Nocturnes" (for piano), Fifth "Barcarolle" (piano), "Second Piano Quartet",[5] "Thémes et Variations",[5] (piano) "Requiem"[5] "La Chanson d'Eve" *(Eve's Song)*[7] "Le Parfum Impérissable" *(The Undying Fragrance),*[4] "First Cello Sonata",[6] "Second Piano Quintet",[6] "Penelope",[9] "L'Horizon Chimérique" *(The Chimerical Horizon,* songs),[6] *"Mirages",* songs,[6] "Second Violin Sonata",[6]

[2] In second volume of his "Mélodies, published by Hamelle, Paris.

[3] In the second volume of his "Mélodies", published by Hamelle, Paris.

[4] In third volume of his "Mélodies", published by Hamelle, Paris.

[5] Published by Hamelle, Paris.

[6] Published by Durand et Cie, Paris.

[7] Published by Heugel, Paris.

[8] Published by Schirmer, New York.

[9] Fauré's only opera; a masterpiece which a poor libretto and inadequate orchestration may banish from the stage. It is published by Hamelle.

"First Piano Quintet",[8] "Thirteenth Nocturne" (piano),[6] and the "String Quartet".[6]

In conclusion, may I cite a few of the shorter phrases or themes. Their beauty speaks so eloquently as to make all comment superfluous, and, after all, citation is the only satisfactory manner of writing about music.

110

Of all his disciples, Roger-Ducasse is the one who was and still remains closest to the spirit of Fauré.

His work is full of emotion, but, at times, one must seek to find it, for it is concealed beneath the somewhat objective brilliance and richness of his style and is held well in control by a mind of unusual power that takes especial delight in clarity of form and solidity of musical construction. One is tempted to apply to him Maurra's sentence about the Greeks: "Feeling pervaded and troubled their conduct, but it was reason which they placed on their altars". *(Le sentiment agitait toute leur conduite, et c'est la raison qu'ils mirent sur leur autel.)*

The "Sarabande", one of the most moving works written in the period we are studying, the "Piano Quartet", the "Pastorale for Organ" and the "Spring Nocturne" for orchestra — to mention

111

only a few titles — are full of tenderness and are manifestly the product of a deep, strong personality. He who would become acquainted, from a different angle, with its force and its charm, has only to read the article[1] which Roger-Ducasse wrote on the chamber music of Fauré, for it gives many an illuminating insight into the quality and penetration of his mind and into the beauty of the relationship which bound him in lifelong affection to his "master".

We turn now to Ravel and Schmitt.

Maurice Ravel, born 1875, because of the almost miraculous perfection of his technique, has been called the "Swiss watchmaker" of modern music. He is the perfect example of the "maître", in the sense that conception and execution seem to represent for him but a single creative process. He can do what he likes. Whatever task he sets himself — whether it be to write a virtuoso work, like "La Valse", for full orchestra, an unaccompanied "Sonata for Violin and Cello", or a song like "Ronsard á son âme" *(Ronsard to his Soul)* where a long, tenuous line of open fifths, played by a single hand, suffices to accompany the voice — is accomplished with astonishing ease and mastery. His command over the manifold resources of the orchestra is prodigious and he moves with facility and evident delight in the most dangerous realms of orchestral virtuosity.

For many people, Ravel is still a lesser Debussy, a mere shadow of the great impressionist. The mistake is understandable but quite unjust to Ravel. There are, to be sure, obvious points of contact between the two men: their mutual repudiation of romantic "eloquence", their veneration for Rameau and Couperin, a common inclination to exoticism and certain similarities of harmonic technique and of piano and orchestral writing. But, nevertheless, the styles of the two composers remain distinct and, what is more important, their personalities differ profoundly.

In spite of the modern character of his style, and in spite of his many works in the impressionistic manner[2] (e.g. "Jeux d'Eau", *Fountains*; "Gaspard de la Nuit", *Gaspard of the Night*; "Trois Poèmes de Mallarmé", etc.), Ravel's deepest affiliations are with the eighteenth century. He has its love of sharp outlines, of concise and lucid form, no little of its ironic wit and humor (e.g. the "Histoires Naturelles", *Stories from Nature*; and "L'Heure Espagnole", *The Spanish Hour*) and his music, like that of the clavecinists, springs from the dance,[3] incarnates its spirit of vivacious movement, its "ever new and delightful pleasure in a useless occupation".

The quotation, which serves as motto to the "Valses Nobles et Sentimentales", suggests another eighteenth-century aspect of Ravel's art, namely, its exquisite delight in the world of elves and fairies. The fantastic and chimerical have always fascinated artists and probably always will, for they are part of the eternal romanticism of the human spirit. The trait itself, therefore, is not characteristic of

[2] But not the least salient feature of even these works is the clarity of their key-scheme and the precision of their form.

[3] e.g. "Menuet Antique", "Alborada del gracioso", "Valses Nobles et Sentimentales", "Sonatine", "Le Tombeau de Couperin", "Trio", "Rapsodie Espagnole", and "La Valse", etc.

[1] In the 1922, October number of the *Revue Musicale*.

any one epoch. Nevertheless, one feels that Ravel's appreciation of the fantastic is more akin to the spirit of Perrault's "Fairy Tales" than it is, say, to Hugo's "Djinns" or to the sumptuous and exotic color of "The Golden Cock". Fairies, for Ravel, are the pretext for a fine and aimless vagabondage of the mind rather than a spur to the curiosity of the sensibility. All his fancies are tinged with a quaint whimsicality, a certain intellectual quality of playfulness that is given very well by these lines from Madame d'Aulnoy's "Green Serpentine", which appear as sub-title to one of the pieces in the "Mother Goose Suite" and which are dedicated to "Little Miss Ugly, Empress of the Pagodas":[1] "She undressed and entered her bath. Immediately little idols began to sing and play. Some had theorbos made of nutshells, others, viols, made from the husks of almonds—for it was necessary to proportion the instruments to the size of the performers".

Finally, Ravel belongs to the eighteenth century by virtue of his reticence. As Roland-Manuel, the composer's gifted disciple and friend, has said: "It is not necessary to know Maurice Ravel personally nor to have penetrated very far into the essentials of his thought to convince oneself that the methods of this musician, his technique and, indeed, his entire art imply a process of voluntary research and the distrust of inspiration. . . . If his music pleases, moves you, or calls forth your tears, know that it was composed by a man who dropped to his knees neither "before nor after', who did not weep in writing it and who, like a certain great poet, thinks that 'he who would write his dream, owes it to himself to be infinitely alert and awake' ".

Not that Ravel's music is without life or feeling. On the contrary, phrases like the following:

[1] "Laideronette, Impératrice des Pagodes."

and many others, are as suave and chaste in their lyricism as the purest molodies of the classics. But on the whole, however, Ravel tends to be objective and the beauty of his music, disdaining the facile confidences of romantic art, resides in the style itself rather than in any qualities of "expressiveness".

Florent Schmitt was born in Lorraine (1870) and his music shows clearly the traces of his double Latin and Teutonic heredity. Clarity and balance of form, sensuous harmonies, acute sensitiveness in matters of sonority, in short, traits which we usually think of as being more or less Gallic, alternate or unite with the more Germanic ideals of ponderous force, of imposing construction and of abundance and depth of feeling.

Being of fiery and impetuous temperament, Schmitt naturally revels in the world of rhythm and many are the contributions which he had made to this aspect of modern music. As early as 1908,

to take but a single example, we find him, in the last movement of the *Piano Quintet,* wielding a type of metre, based on unequal measures, that was later to become a marked feature of Stravinsky's style.[1]

He delights and particularly excels in rhythms of nervous force and movement which, like the following,

become positively sinister by virtue of their insistence and whose violence and abandon often, as in "Orgies",[2] rise to the point of frenzy.

---

[1] Schmitt, however, cannot be said to have "influenced" Stravinsky.

[2] Also from "Antony and Cleopatra": Symphonic preludes and interludes for the drama, after Shakespeare, by André Gide.

[1] Notice the measure of 2½ beats.

There is something titanic about the man. Not only his rhythms, but his themes, so long in line and so lavish of emotional intensity, his luxuriant harmonies, the extraordinary opulence of his counterpoint and last, but not least, the barbaric splendor and color of his orchestra all point to a personality of more richness and power than is usually granted even to men of genius. Instinctively, therefore, Schmitt turns for expression to the grandiose, the ponderous and the mighty. He erects those gigantic and monumental constructions like the "Psalm",[1] the "Piano Quintet" and "Antony and Cleopatra", which, coming from a feebler pen, would be "as sounding brass and tinkling cymbals", but which, at his hands, have acquired the overwhelming force and that sense of inevitability which only the very great can achieve.

Yet one feels that, after all, it would be impossible to imprison within the pages of even such scores the tumult and the torment of a soul like Schmitt's. For the man is fundamentally insatiable. He is athirst for the infinite and no matter how far he may push his lust for intensity of feeling, one knows in advance that he will never quite reach the limit of his desires, that there will always be something more that remains ungiven, unexpressed. And in this abundance of reserve strength lies the chief secret of his power.

In the work of such a temperament, one might expect to find that note of ironic bitterness and disillusion which so often accompanies the sense of human defeat. But with Schmitt's music, such is not the case. To the composer of "The

Tragedy of Salomé" has been given the rare privilege of rendering the torture of a soul in exile without ever, in so doing, falling into the snares of a futile and destructive pessimism. The immense suffering and solitude which are the glorious lot of every genius, have been sublimated by Schmitt into a life of impetuous and creative activity: no one, more than he, arouses in us the love and need of living to the full the brief span of our existence. To a generation which (by a reaction that, in its day, was necessary) was given the taste for "precious" trifles and rare sensations, Schmitt's solid and impassioned music offers the opportunity of dwelling, for a moment, in those high, free regions where, if to suffer means to live more intensely, even suffering is a joy. Hence he belongs among the leaders of men, among those who have brought us light and consolation.

A single quotation from "Dreams",[2] to illustrate the richness of Schmitt's style and to justify the plea that his works be given the more frequent hearings and the wider recognition which their greatness merits.

Albert Roussel, born 1869, took up music as a profession relatively late in life. Only in 1894 did he abandon his earlier career of a naval officer and come to Paris, at the age of twenty-five, to study harmony, counterpoint, fugue and composition, first with Gigout, and later with d'Indy at the Schola Cantorum. All his works bear, in indefinable manner, the evidence of his late start, of a discipline accepted only after the most supple of his formative years were passed. This circumstance of his education explains,

[1] For chorus, soprano solo, organ and orchestra.

[2] For orchestra.

116

perhaps, a certain awkwardness in his harmony, an awkwardness which has nothing to do with the dissonance or modernity of his idiom and which is far more a source of individuality than it is a handicap.

But a personality of Roussel's force needed no external, fortuitous strokes of fortune to develop and fix its natural originality. In all contemporary French music there is no more independent spirit than he and it is exceedingly difficult to trace the influences which assisted in the formation of his language. The "cellular" treatment and "cyclical" form of an early work like the "Trio" op. 2 (1902) are

117

doubtless reminiscent of those severe principles of musical form embodied in d'Indy's monumental "Treatise on Composition".

But the years which Roussel spent in India when he was still an officer of the navy, and his visit to the Orient in 1909-10 were certainly of greater formative significance than the influence of any of his teachers. He is the most exotic of French composers in the sense that his exoticism represents something more than a simple curiosity of a sensibility ever on the alert for new experiences, new sensations. The orientalism of a work like "Padmavati",[1] for instance, is not con-fined to external touches of local color, to the facile effects of a strange and foreign atmosphere. It penetrates to the depths of the Eastern spirit, is saturated with that sense of fatality, of immobility and nonexistence that veils and obscures the savage intensity of oriental instincts and desires. The following phrase, so extraordinary for its feeling of dreamlike volubility, is quite typical of this side of Roussel's temperament and will serve also to illustrate his thoroughly natural use of oriental idioms. Both the melody and the accompaniment of the entire passage, from which I cite only a few bars, is based on the unaltered notes of this scale:

_____
[1] An "opera-ballet".

118

It is not easy to make Roussel's acquaintance, because his language is so essentially orchestral, that piano transcriptions give little idea of its beauty or its power. There is also this difficulty, namely, that modern ears are relatively unaccustomed to listening to music conceived melodically rather than harmonically, and Roussel's idiom, even when it is homophonic, is distinctly "horizontal". To appreciate it, therefore, one must hear it "horizontally", must follow lines rather than chords.

Roussel has yet to receive the recognition and fame that are due him. His fine and delicate ballet, "The Spider's Feast", is fast becoming a modern classic, but his "Evocations",[1] "For a Spring Fête"[1] and "Padmavati", are still, in spite of occasional performances, relatively unknown, even in France. Yet, as these few measures testify,

the man has developed an extraordinarily personal style which cannot be confused with that of any other living composer and one can say, with little risk, that his work promises to hold an increasingly important place in contemporary music.

Honegger, Poulenc, Milhaud, Auric, Durey and Mademoiselle Tailleferre will probably, merely as a matter of convenience, be known for some time as "The Group of the Six". Yet as far as their aesthetics are concerned, they have little in common except a general tendency toward a more or less objective view of their art, a tendency which is characteristic of most recent music and which Roland-Manuel has in mind when he says that "It is no longer the driver who interests us, but the machine which he has set in motion". (*Ce n'est plus le mécanicien qui nous émeuvra, c'est la machine qu'il aura mise en marche.*)

Following, to some extent, in the footsteps of Erik Satie, — an uneven composer, but not without originality and genius — and even more out of absolute necessity, for it was the only thing to do,

[1] For orchestra.

these young composers have tried to react against musical impressionism. But each one has reacted in his own way. Milhaud has done interesting experiments in jazz rhythms and polyharmony (viz., the simultaneous use of two or more keys). Auric and Poulenc, especially the latter, have striven for extreme simplicity, have restored to music, as Ravel did more significantly and in other ways, the pleasure of being just music, that is, a succession of agreeable sounds composed without any thought of subjective or dramatic expression. Poulenc's work, as one can see from these few bars of the opening movement in the "Suite for Piano",

is full of charm. It bears unmistakably the stamp of a born musician and has all the exquisite freshness and spontaneity of youth, for the composer is still but a young man. Consequently, it is too early to attempt any judgment as to the ultimate significance of his work, for, to do so, would be to make prophecies about music that is still to be written. But of the reality and worth of Poulenc's gifts, there can be no doubt.

The most important figure in the group is unquestionably Arthur Honegger. Though he was born in Le Havre (1892) and received the greater part of his musical education in France, Honegger is of Swiss origin and a Swiss subject. He has a quite extraordinary capacity for musical assimilation. Bach, Handel, Wagner, Debussy, Schoenberg and Stravinsky have all contributed to the formation of his language, a language which, because of the very catholicity of the composer's culture, is still in process of evolution. One feels instinctively that the real, the best Honegger is yet to come with his steadily advancing acquisition of a perfected and more highly personal idiom.

He has himself summed up the guiding principles of his aesthetics in a letter which he wrote in September, 1920, to the music critic of "La Victoire". "I attach great importance to the architecture of music and would not like to see it sacrificed to considerations of a literary or pictorial order . . . . My great model is J. S. Bach . . . . I do not, like certain anti-impressionist musicians, seek a return to harmonic simplicity. On the contrary, I feel that we should use the harmonic materials created by the school which preceded us, but that we should use them in a different way, as a basis for lines and rhythms".

On the whole, Honegger has lived up to these principles which seem to augur a return to the objectivity and formal beauty of classic music. His works are characterized by power of construction, richness of polyphony, athletic rhythms and contrapuntal dissonance, that is, dissonance which results from the shock of melodic lines rather than the structure of chords.

It is difficult to say just why Honegger's idiom is personal, for there is nothing about his style which distinguishes it definitely from that of his contemporaries. Lyric in character, it remains so even when the objectivity of the theme[1] would seem to preclude all possibility of lyricism and one is at a loss to explain the directness of the power which it exercises over us. From a work like "King David",[1] there radiates a sort of magnetic energy that escapes analysis, that seizes upon and holds the imagination with all the suddenness and tenacity of a Handelian chorus and which establishes at once the greatness and permanence of the work.

Honegger's chief compositions are written for the orchestra: "Summer Pas-torale", "Horace Victorious", "Prelude for *The Tempest*", "Song of Joy", and "Pacific 231". With the exception of the "Summer Pastoral" (which is relatively homophonic and not, therefore, fully typical). they lose their distinctive merits when transcribed for piano. The vigor and complexity of the counterpoint disappear in the evanescent, uniform sonority of a percussion instrument. But "King David", which brought the composer quick and well deserved fame, is, for the most part, more amenable to transcription and can be domesticated with equal pleasure and profit.

The following measures from a "Cortège" in "King David" offer a fair example of his more dissonant manner and are likewise interesting for their successful superposition of four different keys: F minor, F# major, D minor and E minor.

[1] As in "Pacific" where even the mechanistic becomes a pretext for lyricism.

[2] A "dramatic poem" for chorus, organ and orchestra.

Pierre Menu (1896-1919) is little known, for he died when only twenty-three years of age. But by virtue of that mystery which so often permits those who disappear young to express themselves with authority at an age when most people are still seeking their way in life, he gave the impression of having already quite found himself and one could not help but be impressed by the amazing maturity of his character and his art. In five brief years, from 1914 to 1919, he wrote, during all the anguish and turmoil of the war, a series of works, almost any one of which would ordinarily have been sufficient to gain him distinguished recognition, for all of them bear the indefinable but certain mark of genius. To speak adequately of the qualities which they reveal — their originality, their prodigious technical mastery, the extraordinary power of expression which makes them vibrant with life, the rhythmic force, the rich harmonies and, most of all, their deep tenderness and humanity — would require far more space than we have at our disposal. Fortunately, however, the music itself is so eloquent that, if given the more frequent performance which it merits, it will speak in its own name and will do far more for the memory of Pierre Menu than any testimonies of admiration.

I shall leave to another the task of commenting on the music of my sister, Lili Boulanger (1893-1918).

"In every page of her work, this young girl conciliates the grave power, the authority and rhythmical energy of a man with a certain joyfulness, with the faculty of tender reverie suddenly carried to the point of violent and impassioned anguish; that is to say, with traits characteristic at once of a woman who has divined all the tragedies of the human heart and of a child as innocent and as bent by fate as the poor little princess Maleine whose destiny, a symbol of her own, she sought to interpret.[1] Between her soul and ours there is no intermediary; one does not stop to think of technical procedure, of study or talent. The sonorities awaken — and instantaneously a poetry and a sensibility impose themselves upon us with imperious and persuasive gentleness. Even when Mademoiselle Boulanger is commenting on the verses of another, it seems as though the words were her own. So perfectly does she adapt herself to them, that she remoulds them, gives them new meaning."

The musician who, in a few years, composed "The Three Psalms", "Faust and Helen", "Rifts in the Sky" (*Clairiètes dans le Ciel*),[2] the "Hindu Prayer",[3] and "Princesse Maleine", not to mention ten other compositions, no one of which is of indifferent value, is not a beginner of doubtful promise, but a creative spirit who has accomplished a task and won a place.

"The exquisite and intense figure of Lili Boulanger, facing, without flinching, her terrible destiny, ennobling with her charity the hours which she knew were inexorable, will not move only musicians. She deserves to have symbolic value for all artists and writers who bow with pity and respect before the mystery of premature departures".[4]

---

[1] The reference is to her unfinished opera, "Princesse Maleine" on a text by Maeterlinck.

[2] Songs.

[3] For chorus and orchestra.

Of the many gaps in this brief essay and of its manifest shortcomings, I am only too conscious. It ought rather to have been entitled "A Few Figures in Recent French Music", for the composers whom we seem to have forgotten in it are so numerous and many of them so distinguished that it is better not even to mention them, but to leave to my readers the duty of supplying names and data with which they are all familiar.

By way of conclusion, I could do no better than to quote a paragraph of a recent

letter from Roussel, which sums up with clarity and precision what would seem to be the main directives in the latter part of the period we have been studying. "The tendencies of contemporary music", says Roussel, "indicate a return to clearer, sharper lines, more precise rhythms, a style more horizontal than vertical; to a certain brutality, at times, in the means of expression — in contrast with the subtle elegance and vaporous atmosphere of the preceding period; to a more attentive and sympathetic attitude toward the robust frankness of a Bach or Handel; in short, a return, in spite of appearances and with a freer though still somewhat hesitating language, to the traditions of the Classics."

---

[4] From Camille Mauclair's article on "The Life and Works of Lili Boulanger," in the 1921, August Number of the *Revue Musicale*.

Debussy: The Preludes

J'adore l'indécis, les sons, les couleurs frêles,
Tout ce qui tremble, ondule, et frissonne, et chatoie,
Les cheveux, et les yeux, l'eau, les feuilles, la soie,
Et la spiritualité des formes grêles;

Albert Samain

Le désir seul donne la beauté aux choses.

Anatole France

CLAUDE DEBUSSY was born August 22, 1862, at Saint-Germain-en-Laye, a small town but a few miles out of Paris and in the Ile-de-France, the province where French traditions of taste and culture and commonly said to be the purest. His family was apparently not musical and his father planned to make a sailor of him. Consequently, the boy had no musical instruction until 1871, when, during a visit to his aunt, at Cannes, he took some piano lessons from an Italian named Cerutti, who saw in him no signs of exceptional talent. A little later Debussy made the acquaintance of Charles de Sivry, a brother-in-law of Verlaine and a composer of light operas. It was de

Sivry's mother who, just about the time her daughter was separating from Verlaine, divined the unusual musical talent of the boy who was later to write some of his greatest songs on poems by her son-in-law. She declared that Debussy must become a musician and took charge herself of his elementary musical education. She must have performed her task creditably, for, in the fall of 1873, Debussy was able to enter the Paris Conservatory and continue his studies there under Lavignac, Marmontel and Guiraud. The first three years, he won medals in solfeggio; in 1877, a second prize in piano; in 1880 a first prize in accompaniment, but, curiously enough, he was never given any distinction in harmony.

During the summer of 1879, Debussy went to Russia as family pianist to Madame Metch, the wife of a Russian civil engineer. The influence of this trip on Debussy's musical development has probably been somewhat exaggerated. Many critics are inclined to regard it as having been the composer's "road to Damascus", the capital and decisive point in his artistic development. That he heard in Russia some of the works of Borodin and Rimsky-Korsakov is a least probable (though these composers were relatively little known at this time) and we know that he was impressed by the freedom and abandon of Russian gypsy music. But with the music of Moussorgsky he did not become acquainted until later.

On his return to Paris, Debussy continued, of course, his studies at the Conservatory. Guiraud, his professor of composition, appears to have realized something of the extent and significance of the boy's talents and gave him no little individual counsel and encouragement. Under Guiraud's wise guidance, Debussy made rapid progress and a few years later (1884) won, with his cantata "The Prodigal Son", the much coveted Prix the Rome.

From Rome, in accordance with the regulations, Debussy sent back to the Institute as proofs of his industry: the first part of an opera based on Heine's *Almanzor*; "Spring", a suite for orchestra and chorus without text; a "Fantaisie" for piano and orchestra and "The Blessed Damozel" a work for chorus of women's voices, soli and orchestra, after the well-known poem by Dante Gabriel Rossetti. But this last composition was not finally completed until after his return to Paris.

In 1889 Debussy made a trip to Bayreuth and was greatly moved by performances of "Tristan", "Meistersinger" and "Parsifal". Shortly afterwards, however, a friend showed him a copy of Moussorgsky's "Boris Godounow" — in its original form, that is, before it had been "corrected" by Rimsky-Korsakov. Debussy was struck by the simplicity of the music, its freedom from operatic oratory, but he seems to have been even more impressed by the directness of the style in "Without Sunlight", a group of songs by the same composer. Just how clearly he recognized the obscure affinity which doubtless exists between his own and Moussorgsky's sensibility, we cannot say. But we know that when he returned, the following year, to Bayreuth, the spell was broken. In the light of the new insights which Moussorgsky's music had given him, Wagner seemed heavy, grandiloquent and incompatible, therefore, with the characteristic qualities of the French temperament, to which clarity, proportion and taste are a spiritual necessity.

Nothing is more astonishing in the personality of Debussy — a personality of brutal force and almost savage instincts — than its deep and insistent desire for refinement. During the years in Rome, Debussy was profoundly unhappy, largely, perhaps because of the inadequacy of his culture, which prevented him from revelling, as one might have expected him to do, in the rich atmosphere of Roman antiquity and the Italian Renaissance. On his return to Paris he set resolutely to work, reading voraciously, frequenting poets, painters and visiting picture galleries and expositions; in short, doing everything which seemed humanly possible to fill in the gaps left by his insufficient education. As a result of these efforts, he gradually acquired a culture of extraordinary breadth and subtlety which permitted him to move, and to feel at home, in the most refined and intelligent circles of Parisian society.

The man had the rare knack of recognizing his spiritual ancestors at first sight, of knowing just where to turn for stimulus when stimulus was needed. The same infallible instinct which perceived his artistic kinship with Moussorgsky and which realized so clearly the dangers to a Frenchman of the Wagnerian influence, led him with equal insight to the symbolist and impressionist poets and painters. From about 1890 and 1895 Debussy was a frequent visitor at Mallarmé's apartments in the rue de Rome where, on Tuesday evenings, the great leader of the symbolists received his ever widening circle of disciples and friends. To these gatherings came: Jules Laforgue (for whom Debussy had particular affection, though he never set any of his poems), Gustave Kahn, Stuart Merrill, Henri de Régnier, Pierre Louÿs (author of the "Chansons de Bilitis"), Degas, Whistler, Verlaine (sixteen of whose poems were set to music by Debussy), and others; a choice but heterogeneous company of spirits, held together, for a time, at least, by their common admiration for Mallarmé, by the charm of his personality and the incomparable lucidity of his mind and conversation.

"One entered the room", writes André Gide, "it was evening and you noticed first the extreme silence of the place. The last faint noises of the street died away as one crossed the threshold. Then Mallarmé would begin to speak in that low, musical, unforgettable tone of voice. Strange to say, he thought before he spoke. In his presence and for the first time, one had the impression of touching, as it were, the reality of thought itself. And silently, insensibly and of its own accord, the conversation would rise to heights of almost religious solemnity".

One can easily imagine what such hours in such company meant to a sensitive spirit like Debussy; and of the kind and extent of their influence, we shall have occasion, a little later, to speak in some detail. It was great and wholly valuable and it was indeed fitting that Debussy, in 1892, should have dedicated to Mallarmé his first important work for orchestra, the "Prélude to the Afternoon of a Faun" (*Prélude à l'Après-Midi d'un Faune*).

For nine years, from 1893 to 1902, Debussy worked on his one and only opera, "Pelléas and Mélisande". That he should have chosen Maeterlinck's drama for his text is a tribute to his literary insight and another example of his marvellous knowledge of his own nature and its artistic requirements. The deep humanity of the music; its restrained intensity of expression; the ease and naturalness of a diction which has taken over all the subtle inflections and rhythms of prose, and which is neither speech nor song, but both at once; and, finally, the marvellous unity of atmosphere that pervades the music from beginning to end — an atmosphere heavy with the sorrow and mystery of human life and oppressive, at times, with its burdening sense of man's helplessness before the dark forces of destiny; all these things combine to make the work one of the most extraordinary pieces of lyric drama that has ever been written.

Historically, "Pelléas" represents an almost complete revolution in operatic technique. In it, Debussy both raised and solved the problem of a symbolistic music drama and solved it so well that nothing more remains to be done in that direction. It would be indeed difficult for a composer to write another opera based on the same conceptions as "Pelléas", just as it will be impossible, in the future, to ignore its many and far-reaching innovations. It is truly a pity that so many excellent musicians have yet to make acquaintance with a work which has its place beside Monteverdi's "Orpheus", "The Marriage of Figaro", "Tristan" and "Boris", as one of the few really great operas in the history of music.

Other important compositions also date from the period when Debussy was working on "Pelléas":"Fêtes Galantes", first series (1892);[1] "String Quartet" (1893); "Nocturnes:[2] — Nuages, Fêtes, Sirènes" (*Clouds, Fêtes, Sirens*), from 1897-1899; "Chasons de Bilitis"[2] (1898). The orchestral works, "La Mer" (*The Sea*) and "Images" (*Gigues, Iberia* and *Dances*

of Spring) are later, appearing in 1905 and 1911, respectively. Deserving of more than the mere casual mention which, for lack of space, we are obliged to give it here, is "The Martyrdom of Saint Sebastian", incidental music for a "Mystery Play" by d'Annuzio, some numbers of which the composer later arranged into an orchestral suite. Except in certain pages of "Pelléas" and in the first two "Ballads of François Villon" (1910) — which are likewise far too little known — Debussy had never before attained to heights of such serenity and pathos.

All the well-known piano works, apart from the early and rather sentimental "Suite Bergamesque" (1890), appeared after 1900, beginning with "Pour le Piano" (*For the Piano*) in 1901, and leading up to the two volumes of "Préludes" (1910) and the "Études" (1915).

Debussy's last compositions are frankly inferior. But this is not strange, since they were written under the strain of the war and the steady progress of an incurable disease. André Suarès has described, in moving lines, the man's last appearance in public. "He was paying out of his own purse", says Suarès, "his admission to a charity concert at which some of his works were being given. . . . He had just been very ill and people said he was doomed. He was; for, a short time later, he fell again into the clutches of the malady that was to kill him. I was struck not so much by his thinness as by his air of absence, his appearance of gravity and lassitude . . . In his eyes, which avoided all contacts,

[1] For orchestra.
[2] Songs.

126

one recognized that desperate irony which men who are soon to depart this life have for those whom they leave behind. Between such people there is already such an abyss. That day, whatever one may suppose or whatever may have been his own hopes for himself, Debussy said his farewell." He died, after months of struggle and suffering on the thirty-first of March, 1918.

Émile Vuillermoz, one of the ablest of French music critics, tells about Debussy an illuminating anecdote which is worth repeating, for it is so pre-eminently characteristic of the way in which the composer approached problems of form. In the light of certain events which it would be useless to recall here, Vuillermoz had been led to write, under Debussy's direction, a sort of manifesto, which summed up the regulative ideas of the composer's attitude toward his art. "With all the zeal inspired by my respect and affectionate admiration for the man, I endeavored", writes Vuillermoz, "to give to my résumé all the clearness, balance and irrefutable logic which so attractive a theme seemed to demand. I took especial care to solder the arguments and to chain my phrases firmly together, so that the arm of an adversary should find no vulnerable spot in my armor. Consequently, I presented to the master a well forged mechanism whose every bolt had been tightened with a wrench.

"To my great embarrassment, Debussy did not seem to appreciate these scruples of a professional adjuster. After giving his approval to the ideas which formed the nucleus of my work and after appreciating the logic of their sequence, he begged me, with ironic gentleness, to remove all the artifices of style which as-sured the solidity of the construction, to loosen the pitiless bolts of every conjunctive locution, to abandon the *consequentlys*, the *buts*, the *fors* and the *howevers* which held things together like so many rivets and mortises. He carefully cut what electricians call 'the connections'. Wherever I had sought to tie two propositions together, he intervened and, with a delicate snap of his scissors, set the phrases afloat. Like a master architect who selects and orders his materials so well that he needs no cement for the construction of a vault. Debussy isolated my arguments, gave them air and freedom. And when the task was finished, I could not but recognize that all these 'unharnessed' phrases ran more surely and quickly to their destination than the verbal train whose carriages I had so conscientiously coupled together."

This desire to conceal art by art, to suggest, imply and insinuate rather than to state outright the hidden relationships which guide the sequence of one's ideas, is thoroughly characteristic of Debussy's music and is likewise a master motive in the technique of symbolist and impressionist poetry. There are other obvious points of contact between Debussy and the symbolists and we can consider with profit for a few moments, the common aspects of their art. But in so doing, however, we would do well to remember that both the music of Debussy and the poetry of the symbolists were largely predetermined by certain fundamental ways of thinking and feeling characteristic of the epoch in which they lived, and in which such outwardly contrasting forms of art as the brutal and naturalistic novels of Zola and the delicate, impressionistic poetry of a Verlaine both took their source.

In "Monsieur Croche anti-dilletante",[1] Debussy has occasion to speak of Karl Maria von Weber and suggests that he, Weber, was perhaps the first among musicians to be "troubled by the relationship which must exist between the manifold soul of nature and the soul of nature and the soul of a human being". It would be difficult to state more concisely an idea which, though not new — in France it has been, in one form or another, a source of inspiration to writers ever since the days of Rousseau and Bernardin de Saint-Pierre — was a central notion of the symbolists' *Weltanschauung* and a prime factor in Debussy's own personal attitude toward the world of nature. Your English poet, Byron, in a stanza which Liszt inscribed on the fly-leaf of his "Bells of Geneva", has suggested the same thought from a slightly different angle:

> *I live not in myself, but I become*
> *Portion of that around me; and to me*
> *High mountains are a feeling.*

(Childe Harold III, 72)

But the lines which are usually quoted in this connection and in which the idea is accompanied by the specifically symbolist note of mystery and of sensuous revery, are these verses of Baudelaire:

> *Nature is a temple whose living pillars at times let fall confused words. There man passes through forests of symbols which observe him with familiar glances.*
> *"There — like echoes, which at a distance, mingle into a dark and profound unity, vast as the night and as the light of day — the colors, sounds, and perfumes to each other make answer.*[2]

Beautiful and prophetic lines which foreshadow clearly the manner in which the changing, sensuous beauty of the spectacle and, most of all, the mystery of man's relationship to it were to fascinate and tease the minds of the symbolists. For a Mallarmé or a Samain, so strange and obscure is the nature of man's part in it all, that one cannot hope to state, or even to describe, the quality of the relationship. It is too dark, too subtle and eludes all efforts at analysis.

Yet man's sense of his kindship with the outer world is deep and ineradicable. He feels, though he does not understand it. It is a matter of instinct rather than of reason. Consequently, if he would draw aside the curtain and look beyond, the poet must abandon, for a moment, the ordinary processes of thought, sink back into the realms of the subconscious and trust for temporary guidance to the obscure, spontaneous movements of the soul and to the warm immediacy of sense perception.

Then and then only can he paint the beauties of the outer world and at the

---

[1] The title of the volume in which Debussy published some of the critical articles which he wrote for the *Revue Blanche* and *Gil Blas*, in 1901 and 1903, respectively. In these essays, quite bristling with irony and paradox, he affirms, as one might expect him to do, his predilection for works of taste and refinement, for such men as Mozart, Couperin, Raineau, Watteau and Racine.

[2] *La nature est un temple où de vivants piliers*
Laissent parfois sortir de confuses paroles;
L'homme y passe à travers des forêts de symboles
Qui l'observent avec des regards familiers.

Comme de longs échos qui de loin se confondent
Dans une ténébreuse et profonde unité,
Vaste comme la nuit et comme la clarté,
Les parfums, les couleurs et les sons se répondent.

same time suggest, by the psychological accuracy of his images and the order in which they occur, that dim and distant region where nature and human nature touch, where the objects of the visible world melt, as it were, into their spiritual and human reality and significance.

To be a symbolist, then, is to be an imagist and, more important still, to be a master of suggestion who knows how to throw into the background and, at times, even to eliminate, by a subtle emphasis of their "color" and sound, the too precise and circumscribed concepts which attach to words.

Because of the ineffable mystery of his theme, the symbolist, like Verlaine, dreams of writing "the grey song, in which the precise and the indefinite meet". He avoids, as too harsh and crude, the ordinary uses of words. ("To name an object is to destroy three-fourths of one's pleasure in it.")[1] He has an eye not so much to their actual, as to their possible meanings and prizes them, above all else, for their musicality,[2] their color and sensuousness — in short for their suggestive values.

Naturally, one must not look, in symbolist poetry, for heroic moods, for long impassioned flights of lyricism nor for the cumulative effects of "architecture" and "development".[3] They inevitably have no part in an art which moves in the realms of the subconscious and is based so largely on the fleeting impressions of the senses. The intensity and life of symbolist poetry lie rather in its vividness of imag-

ery and suggestion and if it shuns "construction", it does not, for that reason, become formless. It has form and it has logic, but its logic is the logic of the senses and its form, the form inherent in the natural sequence of sense impressions. In the nature of the case it could not be otherwise.

An art thus based on the fugitive impressions of sense and instinct is peculiarly adapted to rendering those diffused and subtle moods of revery which rise mysteriously to the surface when the mind is silent and the senses alert. The half-shades of the evening with their accompanying sense of the changing and transitory, the languorous melancholy, the silence, mystery, and the magic beauty of the night; — these are the themes which inspire the poems of Mallarmé and his school, poems which, in the words of Rémy de Gourmont, are "the most marvellous pretext for revery that has ever been offered to man".

The statement is equally apt when applied to the music of Debussy, for the latter springs from the same pantheistic view of nature and is the product of a similar technique of sensuous suggestion. The landscape, for Debussy, as it is for the symbolists, is "a state of the soul". He is haunted, as they are, by the desire to render simultaneously its outward and visible beauties and their inner and human significance. Consequently, the marvellous imagery of his music is a means, not an end. For example, what is chiefly remarkable about "Nuages" is not the faithfulness of the picture but rather the manner in which the composer has suggested the melancholy solitude and desolation of spirit which the sight of clouds, drifting slowly and aimlessly

---

[1] Mallarmé.

[2] "Music, first of all." (*De la Musique avant toute chose.*) Verlaine.

[3] "Take eloquence and wring its neck." (*Prends l'éloquence et tords-lui le cou.*) Verlaine.

across the sky, so frequently arouses in us.

Consider, for a moment, the titles of some of Debussy's compositions: "Clouds", "Wind on the Plains", "Reflections in the Water", "The Sea", "Fog", "Goldfish", "Perfumes of the Night". Obviously what attracts him most, as it does the symbolists, is the fugitive and mysterious side of nature.

In the human realm, however, Debussy is drawn in precisely the opposite direction, that is, toward the unreflective, the spontaneous, the involuntary and instinctive. Hence, his predilection for childlike natures, for the dramas of Maeterlinck, whose shadowy characters act less than they are acted upon — by Fate. As Rémy de Gourmont says of them, "they can but suffer, smile, love;

when they try to understand, their troubled efforts give way to anguish and their revolt fades into sobbing. They are climbing, always climbing, the painful slopes of Calvary only to strike their heads against an iron door". In a word, it is the "human" side of nature and the "natural" side of man which particularly interest Debussy. And in this respect he is thoroughly characteristic of his age and generation, the generation of Bergson, that was brought up on Darwin, Taine, Bernard and Renan.

There are also illuminating analogies between certain coloristic aspects of Debussy's music and the technique of impressionistic painting. Take, for example, the opening measures of "Reflections in the Water", where, by the use of the

sustaining pedal, Debussy has blended a whole series of chords into one large, composite stretch of diaphanous sonority. The procedure is quite characteristic of both his piano music and the works for orchestra (where he secures the same effect by *glissandi* on the harp, or by a subtle, overlapping arrangement of the harmonies) and recalls the manner in which Monet, for example, gets his complementary tones and shades by a sharp juxtaposition of little daubs of primary colors which are fused and blended by the distant eye. The resemblance between the

two methods is so striking that the musical device would almost seem to be a direct transposition of the technique of one art into the realm of another. Yet one would scarcely be willing to draw, from such circumstantial evidence, so audacious a conclusion.

Among the specifically musical influences which assisted in the formation of Debussy's style — a style which, in its harmonic aspects, seems at first sight so personal and revolutionary that one might easily make the mistake of thinking that is represents a complete break with the past — we have already had occasion to speak of "Boris Godounov", of the relationship which doubtless exists between the simplicity and directness of Moussorgsky's diction and the free, arioso-like recitative of "Pelléas and Mélisande". Some historians have gone farther and largely on the strength of the resemblance between these measures from "Clouds",

and the following passage from a song in Moussorgsky's "Without Sunlight"[1]

[1] See also these measures from Stravinsky's "Nightingale":

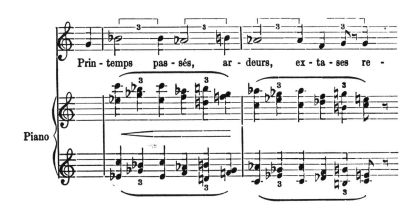

have established a direct and certainly exaggerated connection between the harmonic styles of the two composers. The passage in question may well represent an unconscious reminiscence, on Debussy's part, of a song with which we know he was acquainted. But the fact still remains that the measures from "Without Sunlight" are far more characteristic of Debussy's than they are of Moussorgsky's style. They represent, on the part of the latter composer, one of those mysterious anticipants of the language of a future age, of which there are so many examples in musical history and which have too often tended to provoke controversies that are more amusing than they are illuminating.

The origins of Debussy's harmonic style are to be sought elsewhere; in Liszt, Chabrier and Fauré, rather than in Moussorgsky. The affiliations between Liszt's harmony and the harmony of Debussy are real but somewhat obscure and are most apparent, perhaps, in one or two mutually characteristic ways of connecting triads. The free and expressive manner in which Fauré uses seventh chords is prophetic of Debussy's similar and later use of chords of the ninth. The following cadential formula,

almost an obsession with Chabrier, occurs, in one form or another, again and again in the "Preludes", making the impression of reminiscence unavoidable. Chabrier's influence is likewise apparent in certain arpeggiated forms of melodic line (based usually on the notes of secondary seventh chords) common to both composers and in those sudden lapses into a rather vulgar lyricism and the more popular moods of street song and music-hall to which we shall later have occasion to draw specific attention.

In 1915, Debussy published his two volumes of "Études" for the piano and dedicated them "to the memory of Frédéric Chopin". The inscription is significant, for it represents a conscious homage to the composer whose influence was a chief and guiding factor in the formation of Debussy's piano style.

For many musicians, Chopin's greatness has been somewhat obscured by his rather promiscuous popularity in the concert hall and by the flabby and spineless manner of playing his music which has gradually and insidiously established itself as a "Chopin Tradition". The electric force and abandon of his rhythms, the pride, nobility and martial splendor which are the national heritage of every Pole, have been sacrificed to an effeminate sentimentality which obscures both the refinement and the delicacy, as well as the essential manliness, of Chopin's music.

We shall have to rediscover Chopin, re-appreciate his amazingly original harmonies, the individuality of his piano style with its wide, delicately sonorous spacing of chords, and realize anew the astonishing prophetic qualities of measures like these:

In these final measures of the F major "Prelude", Chopin has dared to add the seventh harmonic to the triad and to treat it as a consonance, as a point of final repose. In that single Eb is implicit all the delicate and sensuous delight in sonorities so characteristic of modern music and to which we shall have frequently to refer in the following commentary on Debussy's Preludes.

VOLUME I.

I. Dancers of Delphos
(*Danseuses de Delphes*)

A slow, stately dance in the simple three part key-scheme found in so many of the Preludes of Bach, namely: Part I, tonic key with inflection, at the end, toward the dominant (measures 1-10); Part II, dominant, with allusions to related keys (11-20); Part III, tonic (21 to the end). Note, in the 18th measure, the delicately sonorous disposition of the harmony and the subtle way in which the timbre of the isolated octaves on C is modified by the addition of the A♭ triad.

II. Sails (*Voiles* — the word is ambiguous and could also be translated *Veils*).

The piece might well have been inspired by some remembered sight of sail-boats drifting listlessly at anchor. It is extraordinary for the vagueness of its atmosphere and the manner in which it suggests — to me, at least — the paradoxical sense of mobility in immobility. With the exception of six measures (based on one of the pentatonic scales: E♭, G♭, A♭, B♭ and D♭), the Prelude is entirely constructed on the notes of the whole-tone scale a scale which, little by little, assumed a rôle of no slight importance in Debussy's work, and whose origins are far back in the past.[1]

[1] The more recent stages in the evolution of the whole-tone scale have been traced by Mr. Hill in his book on *Modern French Music*, p. 201 ff.

III. Wind on the Plains
(*Vent dans la Plaine*)

Obviously a "descriptive" piece, remarkable for the vividness with which the composer has suggested the light, swift-capricious movement of the wind and the silence and the vastness of the plains.

IV. "Sounds and Perfumes Turn in the Evening Air" (*Les Sons et les Parfums Tournent dans l'Air du Soir* — Baudelaire.)

The languor and mystery of a summer night with its accompanying, diffused sense of melancholy and solitude. On page 2, at the points marked "Rubato", are examples of the somewhat vulgar and equivocal lyricism characteristic of Chabrier, to which we have previously alluded. Notice also the originality and mystery of the sonorities in the passage marked "Tranquille et Flottant" and, at the very end, the chords — of such frequent and characteristic occurrence in Debussy's piano music — so vividly suggestive of the timbre of the French Horn.

V. "The Hills of Anacapri"
(*Les Collines d'Anacapri*)

An impression of Italy — the clear and fathomless blue of its sky, the brilliance of its sun, the melodious clang of noontide bells and the nonchalant gaiety, the banal but irresistible romanticism of the Italian street-song. The piece is an interesting example of the way impressionism and realism tend, at times, to merge imperceptibly into one another, a phenomenon so typical of the impressionistic school of painting and also strikingly evident (though in a very different way as far as the emotional effect is concerned) in the work of Malipiero.

VI. "Footsteps in the Snow" (*Des pas sur la Neige*)

An evocation of the melancholy solitude and desolation of a winter landscape. Two pages in which, by the magic of musical suggestion, everything is expressed but nothing said outright and yet which reach the most intimate recesses of the human soul.

VII. "What the West Wind Saw" (*Ce qu'a vu le Vent d'Ouest*).

The tumultuous movement of the sea, lashed and whipped by the fury of the winds. The composer's expression marks — *animated and tumultuous, plaintive and distant, strident, incisive, rapid and furious* — indicate pretty clearly the range of the feelings that dominate the composition, but only the music itself can give any idea of its elemental grandeur and power.

VIII. "The Girl with the Flaxen Hair" (*La Fille aux cheveux de lin*).

Like the *Blessed Damozel*, a "Preraphael-ite" composition, which, had the artist been as much of a musician as he was a poet and a painter, might well have been written by Dante Gabriel Rossetti, the author of these lines:

> *Lady, I fain would tell how evermore
> Thy soul I know not from thy body, nor
> Thee from myself, neither our love
> from God.*

The influence of Chabrier is apparent in the melodic tune of the theme and in the frequent use, in one form or another (measures 9-10, 12-13, 15-16, 18-19, 19-20, 20-21) of the cadential formula which we have previously cited in connection with Chabrier.

IX. "The Interrupted Serenade" (*La Seérénade Interrompue*)

The title alone is sufficient indication of the idea of the piece, which is another example of the use of realistic detail in a composition that is essentially impressionistic in methods and mood. The incisiveness and precision with which Debussy, by a few well chosen strokes of his pen, has attained his end, is amazing.

X. "The Cathedral under the Sea" (*La Cathédral engloutie*)

The work was inspired by an old Breton legend which tells how the town of Ys, swallowed up long, long ago by the sea, rises, at times, from the depths of the ocean and gradually becomes visible in all its ancient grandeur, only to disappear again, a moment later, beneath the waves. Especially remarkable is the manner in which the theme gradually emerges from the misty harmony of the opening measure. Note, too, the specifically impressionistic technique by virtue of which the "primary colors" of successive chords are fused by the pedal into a single mass of hazy, shimmering sonority.

XI. "Puck's Dance" (*La Dance de Puck*)

The flashing lightness and grace of swift, ethereal movement and the mischievous caprice and irony which we associate with the fantastic character of Shakespeare's play. The composer has used extensively the horn-like sonorities which we have already remarked were one of the characteristic features of his piano style.

XII. "Minstrels" (*Minstrels*)

The boisterous humour and facile charm of the music-hall; a mood typical of Chabrier in his "hail-fellow-well-met" vein. What subtlety of observation lurks beneath the apparent facility of so banal a theme and what judgment in the selection of the details to be retained! A few decisive lines, sketched in under the guidance of an eye whose ironic glance seems to be wandering absently over the scene which, in reality, it is observing with pitiless scrutiny, suffice to suggest an entire picture and to establish completely the atmosphere which it evokes.

Only a genius could handle so vulgar a theme successfully. But, after all, in the presence of such a masterpiece, one realizes that, as far as art is concerned, there are no vulgar subjects, but only certain problems which are raised and solved, or not. Here the solution has obviously been found — and with bewildering case and mastery.

Volume II.

I. "Fog" (*Brouillards*)

Vaporous sonorities, hovering uncertainly in the air, from which there gradually emerges a short, phantom-like phrase that is soon lost again in the mists of suspended harmonies. A flash or two of brighter sonorities; then another frag-mentary motive appears — and disappears. The first phrase returns, but once more fades away, in the slowly dissipating fog.

II. "Dead Leaves" (*Feuilles Mortes*)

The vague and regretful melancholy which we associate with autumn and the passing of the summer season. It is one of the compositions in which Debussy's powers of suggestion are at their highest. This chord or that, in a manner now tender, now profound, has a way of making one divine all that the composer would otherwise have kept secret. The diversity of the images, their incessant transformation have been so discreetly insinuated that no detail ever intrudes to break the general outlines of the piece. Misty, yet distinct and spotted here and there with gold, they are ever hovering before our wondering eyes.

III. "The Portal of the Vine" (*La Puerta del Vino*)

Marvellously vivid evocation of popular Spain, of the life in street and tavern, incarnate, as it is here in the spirit of the Spanish dance with all that the latter implies of insolent provocation, of voluptuous abandon and insinuating tenderness, of sudden violence and the sting of sharp desire. The piece was inspired by a mere picture-post-card which Manuel de Falla sent the composer from Spain.

IV. "The Fairies are Exquisite Dancers" (*Les Fées sont d'exquises danseuses*)

Aerial lightness, rapidity and grace; the ethereal sensuousness of an impalpable world of fairy movement and color.

V. "Heather" (*Bruyères*)

A delicate and gracious bit of fancy and autumnal color. The influence of Chabrier is obvious.

VI. "The Eccentric General Lavine" (*Général Lavine-excentrique*)

Debussy's impression of a clown and a delightful piece of pompous humour and burlesque.

VII. "The Terrace where the Moon Receives" (*La Terrace des Audiences du Clair de Lune*)

One of the greatest of the "Preludes" and a miracle of symbolist expressiveness which tempts one to quote the following passage from "Monsieur Croche anti-dilletante". . . . "Music alone has the power to evoke, at will, those imaginary sites and that fantastic but indubitable world which is secretly at work in the mysterious poetry of the night, in the thousand anonymous noises of the leaves, caressed by the rays of the moon."

The title comes from one of the "Indian Letters" which René Puaux wrote for *Le Temps*, but Godet, who divulged the origin of the phrase, is careful not to say whether the music was written before or after Debussy happened to encounter it.[1]

VIII. "Ondine" (*Odine*)

The mobility and seductive grace of the mermaid and one of the many examples on the way in which the charm of flowing water fascinated and inspired the imagination of the composer of the "Preludes".

XI. "Homage to Mr. Pickwick, Esq. P.P.M.D.C." (*Hommage à s. Pickwick, Esq. P.P.M.D.C.*)

A Frenchman's impression of the pompous amiability and humour of Dickens' celebrated character. The mode of gravity in Debussy's citation of "God Save the King" is irresistible.

X. "Funeral Urn." (*Canope*)

The cool and quiet melancholy of a bygone world—suggested by the chaste contours of an ancient urn. The opening measures,

offer a typical example of parallel melodic progression, similar in spirit to the old *organum* and of frequent occurrence in Debussy's music. The feeling of such passages is primarily melodic, the harmonies being rather a by-product of the multiple and parallel melodic lines.

XI. "Alternating Thirds" (*Les Tierces Alternées*)

An *Étude*, whose technical difficulties conceal great delicacy and charm. Notice the long melodic phrase outlined by the upper notes of the first third in every measure. One cannot but marvel at the richness of an imagination which sees in a mere technical problem so many possibilities of delight and beauty.

---

[1] In this and other connections it is interesting to note that Debussy has inscribed his titles at the end, instead of at the head of the "Preludes".

XII. "Fireworks" (*Feux d'Artifice*)

A brilliant piece of pictorial virtuosity, containing, at the very end, an "impressionistic" citation from the "Marseillaise".[1]

Musicians are loath to write about music, too add, as we have done here, verbal commentary to compositions like the "Préludes", compositions whose beauty and poetry speak so eloquently that one is ashamed to have approached them except in silence. One has only to listen to such music to love it and to understand why it is that all nations honor the memory of Claude Debussy and recognize him, not only as the representative of a characteristic moment of French sensibility, but as one of the truly great composers of the world.

---

[1] It would be difficult to read over the "Preludes" without remembering what those who had the good fortune to hear Debussy play have said about his touch. His manner of playing was quite inimitable. So exquisite was the delicacy, the richness of his sonorities, and so masterly were the effects of color which he conjured forth from his pedals, that one forgot that the piano was an instrument with hammers.

Stravinsky[1]

SELDOM have the compositions of any composer provoked such hot debate, such violent hatreds and intense enthusiasms as has the work of Igor Stravinsky. The excitement and tumult which reigned at the first performance, in 1913, of the "Sacred Rites of Spring", an event which is usually referred to as "the battle of the *Sacre*", were such as to make one think one was attending some crucial session of the Chamber of Deputies, some sort of political manifestation rather than a performance of Diaghilev's Russian Ballet.

People shouted, whistled, screamed, stamped and even came to blows over their no uncertain opinions, for it was impossible, in the presence of such music, to remain neutral. The suspended or the lukewarm judgment would have been ridiculous in such an atmosphere. One either loved or hated the music and that was the end of the matter. Now, of course, the work is universally recognized as a masterpiece and its composer is everywhere acknowledged to be the foremost figure in contemporary music and — what is more amusing, in the light of his supposed anarchistic tendencies — the chief representative of a return to classic traditions.

We will not attempt, in so short an article, to trace the extraordinary evolution of Stravinsky's style, for to do so would entail individual discussion of a large part

---

[1] Igor Stravinsky was born at Oranienbaum in 1882. His father was an opera singer, yet, strangely enough, the boy studied first to be a lawyer and it was only at the age of twenty-one, after a meeting with Rimsky-Korsakov, that he abandoned the law and began, under Rimsky-Korsakov's direction, to prepare himself systematically for the career of a professional musician.

of his works, many of which are so distinctive so different from the ones which precede or follow them,[1] that it is peculiarly difficult, and in some cases impossible, to find any logical and illuminating method of arranging them into groups or "periods". The limits of our lecture forbid our discussing the works, in large measure, singly and in detail. Hence we shall simply endeavor to sketch in the general outlines of Stravinsky's art, its underlying tendencies and to give the more important of the influences under which it has evolved.

The chief obstacle which blocks the way to most people's appreciation of Stravinsky's music is its dissonance, for all the works after "Petrouchka" *are* dissonant, some of them, extremely so. And what makes the obstacle especially difficult to overcome is the fact that Stravinsky's dissonance is far more contrapuntal than it is harmonic, that is, it results from the clash of melodic lines rather than the structure of chords. Ever since the days of Haydn and Mozart, our ears have been trained to hear practically in but one direction, that is, vertically and, in consequence, we have more or less lost the art of listening to contrapuntal music, of following lines rather than chords. Even Bach we hear, in large measure, harmonically and are tempted to pay more attention to the vertical concordance, than we do to the contours, of his melodies. Yet, these perpendicular concordances do not, for the most part, have the value of chords, but are rather accidental aggregations of notes —

to call them harmonies would be inaccurate — which have resulted from the conduct of the multiple and independent lines. On the other hand, however, it is true that such concordances constitute a sort of harmonic skeleton. But it is only a skeleton and its presence should be felt rather than perceived and surely not consciously and continually observed by the listener.

In Stravinsky's music, we are not only confronted by counterpoint, but by counterpoint whose vertical concordances are new and which, being new, naturally draw our attention so forcibly to them that we lose sight of the lines which produced them and which ought to be our chief concern. One has but to glance at the measures from "The Sacred Rites of Spring", on the facing page, to realize at once that they are essentially linear in character. In this respect, they are quite typical, for most of Stravinsky's music is pre-eminently melodic and it is interesting to note how his polyphony has passed from the relative simplicity of contrapuntal device which characterizes "Petrouchka" (1910-11), to the more complicated polyphony in "Sacre" (1911-13) and "The Wedding" (1917), only to return to the extraordinary concentration and economy of the "Piano Sonata" (1924).[2]

To appreciate such music, it is obvious that we must establish new habits of hearing, re-acquire a new sense of the old linear values which were the pride of the Renaissance and the glory of Bach.

But there is a greater difficulty in Stravinsky's music, namely, the element of

---

[1] For instance, such radically different works as "The Firebird", "Petrouchka" and "The Sacred Rites of Spring" followed each other in quick succession. They date respectively from 1909-10, 1910-11, and 1911-13.

[2] Notice, in the last example, the use of the old contrapuntal device known as "augmentation".

rhythm, and here the trained musician and the layman are equally embarrassed. For several centuries now, we have lived under the tyranny of the barline, of a "strong" beat which reoccurs at *regular* intervals with insistent monotony. Consequently, we find ourselves helpless when we are forced, as we are so often in Stravinsky's music, to admit another type of rhythm, a rhythm in which the metre is constantly changing and where we are

140

obliged to feel accents at intervals that are no longer regular. Stravinsky's music suggests the old Greek system of rhythm which (instead of taking, as we do, a *maximum* unity, like the whole-note, and cutting it up into various small divi-sions, e.g. halves, quarters, eighths, etc.) took a minimum unity and multiplied it by any even or odd number, 3, 4, 5, 6, 7 etc. This is precisely what Stravinsky does, for instance, in the last tableau of "The Sacred Rites of Spring":

Nor is the example an isolated one; we find the same procedure in a great many of his themes, from which I cite, at random, the following:[1]

[1] It is illuminating to compare the metre of these themes with the metre of the first few lines of a speech in Euripides' Hippolytus:

In both cases the principles of rhythmical structure are obviously the same. For a detailed study of the musical aspect of Greek metres, see Maurice Emmanuel's book: *Histoire de la Langue Musicale*, Paris, 1911.

The difficulty is doubled when, as in this passage from "The Story of the Soldier", Stravinsky superposes rhythms in much the same way as the contrapuntist superposes themes:

One has only to try to play these measures to realize how ill-equipped we are to cope with the rhythmical problems[1] of Stravinsky's music. Yet we shall never fully understand it until we have mastered them, until we have acquired the physical sensation of his rhythms and made them our own.

---

[1] Or even, for that matter, with those presented by the music of Bach. How many pianists, for instance, can play a Bach fugue with perfect clarity, that is, in a manner which makes quite clear the rhythmic, no less than the melodic, independence of the parts.

Stravinsky's music is fundamentally tonal, that is, it gravitates around a "home" key which is usually affirmed, in

no uncertain manner, by a perfect cadence. Occasionally, it is true, there are equivocal measures like these:

which, at a first glance, would seem to be polytonal. Yet in spite of such passages, I do not think that in Stravinsky's case one can properly speak of polytonality. As Boris de Schloezer has said:[1] "There is genuine polytonality where, as in the *Symphonie Études* of Milhaud or in his *Sixth Quartet*, there is complete independence of the tonal planes, independence to such a degree that each voice of a bi-tonal discourse, for example, pursues and finds its own resolution and has its own cadence. This is not the case with Stravinsky, either in the Sacre or in the works which follow it. In Stravinsky's music there is always a strongly affirmed fundamental tonality to which melodic lines and harmonic complexes belonging to a different key temporarily join themselves. But the foreign key is either, in the end, abandoned, or else it melts, in modulating, into the fundamental tonality. . . . Beneath the complexities of a harmonic tissue where two or three differ-

ent keys are woven together, one always distinguishes the plane of the principal tonality, which finally absorbs the others and affirms itself by a cadence which destroys all doubt".

The sort of harmonic perspective which M. de Schloezer describes, is to be found, for instance, in the Prelude to the second part of "The Sacred Rites of Spring". Hence, the fundamental key, D minor, is always in the foreground the foreign tonalities being rigorously confined to secondary planes. Similarly, the frenzied "Dance of the Earth" which concludes the first section of *Sacre* and which likewise contains melodic lines that, like the following,

suggest other keys, is nevertheless, from the harmonic standpoint, nothing but a gigantic cadence in C major. It would be useless to multiply examples further. If any additional evidence were necessary to establish the underlying tonal basis of Stravinsky's music, it could be found abundantly in the later works, each succeeding, one of which indicates an in-

[1] In an admirable article on Stravinsky in the 1923, December number of the *Revue Musicale*. This article and the marvellous essay which Ernest Ansermet wrote on Stravinsky's music and which likewise appeared in the *Revue Musicale* must inevitably serve as the starting point for any study of Stravinsky's work.

creasingly marked evolution toward an art of single sharply defined tonalities.

Like any powerful personality, Stravinsky has absorbed and assimilated the most diverse and conflicting influences. In the early works, we find traces of "The Five"; of Glazounov. (In the Symphony in E*b*, 1905-07), Scriabine and Wagner (*Études,* Op. 7, 1908; and *The Firebird*). Rimsky-Korsakow (*Fireworks,* 1908; and *The Firebird*). Debussy, (*The Faun and the Shepherdess,* 1907, *The Firebird,* and in certain impressionistic, overlapping harmonics in *Petrouchka*), and Schoenberg (*Three Japanese Lyrics,* 1912).

In the compositions written between 1910 and 1917 there is a prolonged and fruitful influence of the Russian folk song, noticeable in the plagal character of the melodies — that is, their insistance of the interval of the fourth — in the diatonic structure and the rhythmical freedom of the themes and in their frequent modal qualities. Often Stravinsky takes his themes bodily from the folk-lore of his country. For example, the following melodies from "The Sacred Rites of Spring",

are all, according to M. de Schloezer (who is Russian himself and a well qualified authority in the matter) of folk origin.

On the other hand, "the themes of *Petrouchka*", says M. de Schloezer, "are not, for the most part, of village or peasant origin; nor are they fundamentally Russian. They represent rather the music of the town, of the city folk, who have already assimilated a good bit of western musical culture, if only in the form of waltzes such as the one by Lahner which occurs in the first tableau of *Petrouchka*. The result is a strange but homogeneous and organic compound of polkas and German waltzes, churned out by a hurdy-gurdy; of gypsy romances, sung by nomad artists, and of Russian dance rhythms. To-day, in the provinces, even after the Revolution, we can distinguish the echoes of this musical life which, ten years after *Petrouchka*, has once more inspired Stravinsky in *Mavra* (1922). The themes of *Petrouchka*, then, are not, properly speaking, Stravinsky's own.... The dances of the drunkards, of the coachmen, of the merchant and the two gypsic — we Russians have known all that since childhood. It is material which belongs to everyone; but Stravinsky, in amalgamating and organizing these diverse elements, has made them his own and given them new value and significance".

In *The Wedding* it is difficult, I confess, to trace the precise limits between the melodies which Stravinsky has created himself and those which he has borrowed from the genius of the folk. In the second tableau, the refrain on a liturgical text that the friends of the groom sing, is in reality a soldier song which in the original has no religious character whatsoever. This phrase of the groom's

144

Et vous père et mè - re bé - nis - sez votre en - fant

is sung in Russia at the mass for the dead. For Stravinsky, it sufficed to make a few almost imperceptible changes to modify its funereal character without destroying the grave, religious quality of the melody.

The importance of the part which his native folk-songs play in his works is only one of the many distinctly Russian aspects of Stravinsky's music. Equally Russian is the Asiatic splendor and color, the unparalleled luxuriance of its orchestration, an art, the elements of which Stranvinsky learned from Rimsky-Korsakov and in which he is unexcelled by anyone. Intensely Russian, also, is the sombre nostalgia, the sullen immobility and that inscrutable sense of fatalism which we find in compositions like "The Firebird", "The Sacred Rites of Spring", "The Wedding" and in the paradoxical tragi-gaiety of "Petrouchka". It would be difficult to imagine a work more genial, more irresistibly gay than "Petrouchka" and, at the same time, more profoundly tragic. I cannot listen to the music without recalling my first impressions of Russia when I visited that country shortly before the war. On reaching the frontier, we found the little station crowded with peasants, some of them alert and expectant, their eyes wide open, sparkling and full of vivacity, in short, happy, gay; others sad, but so sad that they gave you the feeling that human sorrow is, after all, an infinite thing. And in every face one could read the incomprehension of these simple folk, their helpless acceptance of life. Instinctively one realized that their happi-

ness, like their sorrow, was unmotivated. They were simply gay or sad—nothing more. For the rest, well, "nitchevo" as the Russians say, "That has no importance". It was an unforgettable impression.

In the later works "Mavra" (1918), "Pulcinella" (1919) "Ragtime", the "Octet for Wind Instruments" (1923), the "Concerto" (1924), and the "Sonata" (1924) for piano, the Russian folk-song has given way to other influences. In "Pulcinella", for instance, Stravinsky has taken melodies by Pergolese, harmonized them in a distinctly modern style and made them over into something quite new and original. The work is a *pastiche*, if you wish, but a *pastiche* of genius. The "Octet" turns, for inspiration, to the airs of Rossini; "Mavra", an *opera-buffa*, glorifies what de Schloezer wittily calls the "Italo-Tzigano-Russian" romance. And in "Ragtime", of course, it is your American jazz rhythms that form the basis of the music.

Syncopation has always fascinated Stravinsky. There are marked traces of it is "Petrouchka", in "The Sacred Rites of Spring", and it is employed extensively in "The Wedding". But perhaps the most interesting examples of jazz rhythms are to be found not in any of these works, nor in "Ragtime", but in the "Piano Concerto", for here they have been woven into a style of counterpoint which, in spite of its dissonance and modernity, suggests unmistakably and at once, the polyphony of Bach. Strange as it may seem, the fusion results in not the slightest incongruity. It is as effective as it was unexpected.

145

In the "Piano Sonata", his last published work, the influence of Bach is at once subtler and deeper than ever before. The work, like the Preludes and Fugues of the great Cantor, is conceived in blocks and is distinctly architectonic in character. It has no "expressive" intention in the romantic sense of the word. The nuances are very simple, the dynamics consisting, even in the slow movement, only of simple oppositions of *fortes* and *pianos* and an occasional *pianissimo.* On the other hand, differences in touch or attack are sharply contrasted. The left hand, for instance, plays *staccato*, and the right, *legato*, or *vice versa.* The first and last movements, at least half of which utilizes but two voices, one in each hand, may be considered as representing a development and modernization of the two-part, contrapuntal style of writing that we associate with Bach's "French and English Suites". The extraordinary life and interest of the work reside, as they do in Bach's music, in the style itself, in the vitality of lines which are perpetually in movement, are forever unfolding and renewing themselves. In the long history of music, one encounters a great many works of the "mosaic" type, that is, works which proceed by the juxtaposition and variation of short phrases, but extremely rare are compositions where the lines develop from within, grow out of themselves, as they do here, naturally, easily and with inexhaustible fecundity.

Stravinsky is a master craftsman. Each one of his works brings us, in addition to those intense joys which only the supreme works of art can give, the solution of some technical problem, of some difficulty of his "trade" which, in writing his music, he has incidentally mastered. Sometimes he sets the task for himself quite consciously and then we get tiny marvels of craftsmanship like the "Five" and the "Three Easy Pieces for Piano — Four Hands" which are marked respectively "right hand" and "left hand easy". More often, however, I imagine the task is an incidental one, which is accomplished as a matter of course, simply because the realization of his ideas demands that he accomplish it. However that may be, two things are certain: first, that Stravinsky's music has solved many and extraordinarily diverse problems; and secondly, that the man has shown marvellous versatility in adapting his personality to so great a variety of subjects.

From the historical point of view, Stravinsky's music represents a sharp reaction against the subtle and vaporous sonorities of Debussy's impressionism and a powerful impetus in the direction of a return to classic traditions. Ever since the beginning of the nineteenth century, music has beem more or less autobiographical, has dealt with the feelings or impressions of the individual. Its beauty and power have lain in its expressive qualities, in the intensity and fidelity with which it has reflected the emotional life of the composer, rather than in any objective values of form or structure.

In Stravinsky's music, however, the individual or personal note is relatively absent. Consciously or unconsciously he has sought and found again the secret of classic art, of an art whose movement and life are in the music itself, not in any qualities of "expression". Even when he is expressive, Stravinsky remains quite impersonal.[1]

Here he was aided partly, perhaps, by his Russian heredity; for, if one stops to think of Russian opera, for instance, one realizes that the most successful episodes, even in so great a masterpiece as *Boris Godounov*, are rarely personal in character. The greatest scenes usually represent some large, general, collective emotion and excell rather in the more or less objective beauties of the gorgeous and the spectacular. In this respect, "Petrouchka" and "The Sacred Rites of Spring", for example, are thoroughly Russian as well as classic. They deal with the feelings of the group: they speak for the crowd, not for the individual.

For those who happen to know only the *Sacre*, it may seem strange indeed to speak of Stravinsky as a classicist, for the primitivism of *Sacre* or, if you prefer, its naturalism, is certainly not a "classical" tendency. But in this connection, one must remember the circumstances under which the work was written, and must place it in its proper historical setting, namely, against the background of impressionistic and romantic art. As M. de Schloezer has said: "It was necessary to return to nature and to forget man, or, at least, to reduce him to nothing more than an element of primitive nature, to treat him as a rock or a plant. The rudeness of *Sacre*, its disdain for everything which charms or pleases, its stinging brutalities — all that was necessary, for it was a question of killing sentiment, of destroying all subjective emotion and of making things act directly and by themselves". Furthermore, "The Sacred Rites of Spring", is Stravinsky's only excursion into the realm of naturalistic art and occupies, for that reason, a place apart from the rest of his works.

If, as in "The Wedding", Stravinsky again approaches the world of primitive peoples, it is to raise them higher in the scale of human values, to give their humble lives new and transcendent dignity. Here, in *"Noces"*, simple, peasant folk become figures of truly epic grandeur. "The Bride", "The Groom", "The Father", "The Mother" are not obscure individuals but representative types, who speak, in accents as noble as they are touching and profound, for all men and all times. Only to the very great has it been permitted, in the past, to achieve such heights of universal beauty. That Stravinsky should have done so is no small tribute to the greatness of his genius and a certain indication of the classic and enduring qualities of his art.

---

[1] *Generally* speaking. Naturally one can find exceptions to this, as to any other classification. There are "personal" moments in Stravinsky's music just as there are "impersonal" moments in the music of the nineteenth century. But, as a large generalization, the opposition which we have established between the romantic era and the music of Stravinsky is real and easily discernible.

Dissonance is Today
Consonance is Tomorrow

BY NADIA BOULANGER

SOME PEOPLE THINK that composers today are not so able to express their own individualities in what they write as the composers of other eras. Each period has similar virtues. In the whole history of France you have a common language, common technique, but personality emerges in an uncontrollable way — it is there. I find this a very interesting period. Virgil Thomson, Aaron Copland, Roy Harris, Douglas Moore, David Diamond, Walter Piston, Robert Russell Bennett — naturally they reflect the times they were in. I think it has always existed.

Some think the young composers of today try to avoid consonance. But what do we call consonance? You remember when Debussy was a little boy and the secretary of the Conservatory came to him and said, "Have you finished poisoning the ears of your friends with all this dissonance?" And Debussy answered and he was only 12 years old, "Oh Mr. Secretary, dissonance is today. Consonance is tomorrow."

Recently I was asked what I would do if one of my students brought me a "conventional" composition of great beauty. It depends on what you call conventional. Do you make a similarity between tradition and habit? I adore tradition. I cannot stand habit. Simply to repeat is nothing, also to destroy is nothing. Tradition is never interrupted, we are always evolving but never interrupted.

Beautiful music — beauty is outside any other question. There is a difference because nationalities create differences but no superiority. History makes one period near the other; the present depends so much on the past, and on the future.

I was asked if the composer displays more imagination when he is able to write "descriptive" music. We don't write descriptive music in general, we write only music. Whatever the form of music is, it is only a reason to reappraise the real meaning of music with external possibilities.

Is melody lost sight of in preference to dissonance in contemporary composition? Melody has nothing to do with dissonance or consonance. Melody is a line, always a line in music. I don't believe we can ever speak on this. Every

50 years we hear about the death of theatre, and the theatre is perfectly well; it goes on, has never ceased to go on. But one speaks always of decadence because people do not accept the fact that life must evolve.

I am often asked how I teach. One cannot generalize unless one has a plan and I have not a plan. I try to understand who they are. I try to help them, improve their techniques. On any other ground there is no action. If you have no action from the thought of anybody, it means he is not thinking very much.

It is different which each pupil, you cannot compare the development of one with another. You can say that they are equipped to do something or not equipped: and, on this equipment, one can have a certain control. But on nature, one can have no control.

If he is a born composer, he will be a composer. So if you teach people technique they may have the imagination, they may have the creative gift. That you cannot create, you cannot transform it.

Everything is moving constantly, nothing is motionless, nothing is settled. At the same time one must go through the methods, not a system, but the methods which develop a logical mind, a control of this mind, because that is absolutely necessary. Without method nothing can exist. First I believe in preparing a musician to be a good musician.

Someone asks, "Do you associate genius with initiative?" Those are wonderful words. A great mind said, "Talent without genius is a little thing but genius without talent is nothing." This is perfectly true. You have to know the language and if you have no language you can express nothing. And when you have a lot to express, you simply employ the language of everybody.

A student asks, "What are the advantages, if any, of private lessons or class lessons?" You can talk about composition in a class but you cannot really teach composition in a class. I am not sure one can give a class in composition. In a private lesson one can discuss a composition but when people are not ready, nothing can be done. When they are ready you can discuss a point, but you cannot make a composer if he is not a composer. You can give him a language, you can give him a means of expression, but then he must express himself.

Students ask if they should have complete knowledge of orchestration before they come to me. If he is *really gifted*, I would be interested in taking someone who is really a beginner. I cannot say this or that because I don't know. For me, life is moving in such a way that each hour brings something different.

Then they ask, "How can you tell if someone is gifted?" You discover it very soon: in playing, in talking, in what he has done. You feel what his

150

background is, what he knows, what he is thinking of. How can you recognize the spark in a composer? Fortunately, all that is worthwhile escapes through this control. We can't define that with words. We do not know what is beauty, we do not know what is love. We only live under the light of what we know is essential, or nothing means nothing.

One can never train a child carefully *enough*. If you take general education, one learns to recognize colors, to recognize words, but not to recognize sound. So the eyes are trained but the ears very little. This is not because someone taught me that red is not blue that I pretended to become a painter. But most people hear nothing because their ear has never been trained. And many musicians hear very badly and very little.

When I was a child I was terribly shocked when I was told that it says in the Gospel that very much would be given to the one who has received. But today, many years afterward, I understand that it is essential, we must do everything we can for the one who can do very much, and it is unfair to our human justice. But human justice is a small justice.

Someone asked me, "Is there anything in or about the world of music that could be improved?" We can always improve, all our lives. They ask me questions as though I was a prophet. I am only a poor teacher travelling hour after hour, trying to do what has to be done, day after day.

Dieudonné and Boulanger walk arm in arm to dinner, Fontainebleau, 1972. Photo © Douglas Lyttle.

151

FONTAINEBLEAU.   Hommage à Nadia Boulanger

marvi 75

Sketch by Marion Tournon-Brandly.

The production of *Master Teacher: Nadia Boulanger* was supervised by Daniel Connors. The book was designed by Gerard Valerio, Bookmark Studio, Annapolis, Maryland, typeset by Lincoln Graphics, Washington, D.C., and printed and bound by Edwards Brothers, Inc., Ann Arbor, Michigan.